ADVENTURE AWAITS

"*Adventure Awaits* isn't just a how-to on discernment (although it's full of practical advice). It's also not just a memoir (although Stacey Sumereau's story is well worth a read). Rather, it combines the two into a compassionate guide on growing closer to the Lord and surrendering everything to him. Sumereau's beautiful voice shines through on every page, and the wisdom she's gained from her life and the grace of God is golden. I wish I'd been able to read this book years ago!"

Taryn DeLong
Copresident of Catholic Women in Business
and author of *Holy Ambition*

"Stacey Sumereau's life story is a relatable account of the adventure of following God's plan. She writes: 'God isn't a to-do list. God is love.' With plenty of practical tips and encouragement, Sumereau reminds us that God desires our joy even more than we do. Her life is a testament that God is worthy of our trust—and to surrender and follow him leads to true peace."

Maggie Craig
Speaker and author of *Friendship Reset*

"Chock full of spiritual wisdom, personal testimony, and relatable insights. Stacey Sumereau offers a readable treasure to inspire us on our journey toward God wherever our vocation or path might lead."

Jackie and Bobby Angel
Catholic speakers, authors, and YouTubers

"This book is superb! I enjoyed reading it and found myself reflecting on how the transformative experiences in our lives can deepen our connection with God. Stacey Sumereau's honest sharing of how God presented his plan for her life is a wonderful witness to the discernment process. Through her journey of faith, reflections on scripture, and meditative questions embedded throughout the chapters, Sumereau provides us with an opportunity to contemplate how our own life events are a call to cultivate a closer relationship with God."

Sr. M. Peter Lillian Angeline DiMaria, OCarm
Congregational Leadership for the Carmelite Sisters
for the Aged and Infirm

"As a fellow actor, I know Stacey Sumereau's story all too well: allowing my ambitions to drown out God's voice, saying all the right things and doing all the wrong ones, and wearing a hundred different masks for a hundred different people. You don't need to have a flair for the dramatic to feel the same kinds of disconnection in your own heart. I recommend this book for anyone who is daring enough to let God take center stage in their life."

Tanner Kalina
Catholic evangelist and author of *Aching for Greatness*

"An engaging and insightful guide, this book offers practical tools for living life with Christ at the center. Stacey Sumereau's playful yet impactful storytelling invites readers to reflect on their own journey while offering wisdom to discern God's will. It's a valuable read for anyone seeking to grow deeper in faith and understand their God-given purpose."

Heather Khym
Cohost of the *Abiding Together* podcast
and author of *Abide* and *Encountering Emmanuel*

ADVENTURE AWAITS

HOW TO INTERPRET YOUR DESIRES
AND HEAR GOD'S VOICE

MY JOURNEY FROM BROADWAY TO
THE CONVENT TO MOTHERHOOD

STACEY SUMEREAU

Ave Maria Press AVE Notre Dame, Indiana

Founded in 1865, Ave Maria Press is a ministry of the United States Province of Holy Cross.

www.avemariapress.com

Paperback: ISBN-13 978-1-64680-375-0

E-book: ISBN-13 978-1-64680-376-7

Cover images © Getty Images.

Cover and text design by Brianna Dombo.

Printed and bound in the United States of America.

Library of Congress Cataloging-in-Publication Data is available.

CONTENTS

ACKNOWLEDGMENTS

This book has only become possible with the encouragement and dedication of my editor, Heidi Hess Saxton, to whom I am deeply grateful. I am also grateful to the entire team at Ave Maria Press who have tirelessly contributed to this work.

My thanks to my husband John Sumereau and friend Emily Golec who reviewed the book in its early drafts and offered valuable insight and encouragement. Endless thanks to my parents, who were my earliest image of God's love and have continued to love me without measure.

And thank you to my one-year-old, Michael, who always inserted himself with unsolicited comedic relief at the most stressful moments to remind me not to take myself too seriously.

This book is dedicated to my husband, John, and our children Raphael, Azelie, Honora, and Michael. You are my greatest adventure.

INTRODUCTION

Do you feel unqualified to make the big life choices in front of you? Does it feel like everyone else knows where they're going, and you wish you could too? Are you terrified of choosing the wrong job or vocation? Are you slogging through an unimpressive season, feeling like you're wasting time? When I was fresh out of college, I felt all these things. That season reminds me of my brother's experience in the longest river race in the world, the MR340. My brother Tim is a three-time competitor in the MR340. The course is 340 miles of the Missouri River, a stretch spanning Kansas City to St. Louis, Missouri. My brother has finished in the top hundred with a time of about sixty hours. Yes, you read that right: sixty hours of continuous paddling with only brief periods of necessary rest.

Have you ever heard the expression "Life is a marathon, not a sprint"? I disagree. Navigating life decisions can be like thinking you signed up for a marathon, then showing up to discover you're actually in the MR340. You thought it'd be over after twenty-six miles. Now you realize you have to go twelve times farther and somehow find a boat—*joke's on you!*

It's disorienting on the river: the shore is far away, and the finish line is completely out of sight. You find yourself facing one choice after another. It's harder than you ever expected, and you feel totally unqualified to make a decision. Maybe you don't even know what you want . . . and the thought of leaving it up to God scares you even more. What if his will turns out to be the one thing you hate?

I have good news for you! The responsibility to navigate this journey isn't all on your shoulders. Your path is mapped and established by the One who knows and loves you best. He wants to give you everything you need to journey with purpose, passion, and peace.

But wait, you might be thinking. *I've never heard God's voice before. I thought seeing visions and hearing voices was reserved for the great mystics, not me! How am I supposed to figure out what God wants for me—where he wants me to go, what he wants me to do?* I have good news for you there too. Let's return for a moment to my brother's story.

My family and I—eight siblings and our parents—avidly follow Tim's virtual tracking map during his races. It shows his exact location and the percentage he's completed. I've often wished for a tracking map for life! However, God doesn't need GPS to show us his plan: God speaks to those who love and serve him.

Learning to hear God's voice day to day has taught me that his voice, not a map, is my best guide. My hope is that, by reading my story and what I've learned, you'll grow in trust that God is present to you and is taking care of you. Each chapter illustrates a different way that God speaks to us. I hope these "checkpoints" illuminate new ways of finding God's voice and his assistance everywhere around you.

The MR340 website states, "Knowledge is power. In this race, knowledge translates into time, safety, strategic advantage, less suffering and even survival. You can't just show up the day of the race and expect to get all the info you need to finish . . . much less succeed. This race is a stage for you to accomplish the impossible."[1] Leading up to the MR340, Tim invests many hours in training, acquiring gear that will help him achieve a finish, and planning his racing strategy. I wrote this book to be your racing strategy. It'll banish the overwhelm and equip you with the knowledge you need to navigate choices with confidence.

As my brother entered his twenty-fifth grueling hour on the river, I jokingly posted in our family group chat, "I'm doing a fifteen-minute workout this morning in Tim's honor!" Truly, though, do I embrace my life's race toward God as an adventure? Or do I try to do as little as possible—a scant exercise here and there?

The best part of God's adventure is not just doing his will but also fulfilling *your deepest desires*. Yes, you read that right. God wants to give you the deepest desires of your heart. Pere Liagre, CSSp, wrote, "God . . . never inspires the soul with desires that cannot be gratified. He only awakens desires in order to satisfy them, and more completely than we can imagine or ask for."[2] In the following pages, you'll read how I learned to attune my heart to God's voice and tap into my deepest desires. You'll learn how to recognize him working in your story—no matter how messy—and gain confidence and peace.

God's adventure awaits, my friend, and I'm thrilled to be on the journey with you.

TO ENHANCE YOUR *ADVENTURE AWAITS* EXPERIENCE WITH VIDEOS AND OTHER RESOURCES PLEASE VISIT WWW.STACEYSUMEREAU.COM/ADVENTUREAWAITSBOOK.

DIVING INTO SCRIPTURE

LETTING GOD'S WORK BREAK INTO ME

> Listen to my voice; then I will be your God and
> you shall be my people.
> —Jeremiah 7:23

I was hurrying down a busy central street in Manhattan one Tuesday afternoon when I saw the "212" area code light up on my phone. I was in the middle of an exclusive two-week musical-theater intensive hosted by the American Theatre Wing, the organization that runs the Tony Awards. Just that morning I had stood on a Broadway stage for the first time—the Majestic Theatre, home of the iconic *The Phantom of the Opera*—for an acting workshop. Now we were hurrying back to our main studio near Times Square for a seminar.

I knew I wasn't supposed to deviate from my group, but I ducked into a kitschy gift shop to take the call. Having recently graduated from Catholic University's musical-theater program, my dreams of seeing my name in lights had induced me to hop a Greyhound to audition for *The Wizard of Oz* Broadway National Tour in New York City.

More than a thousand hopefuls showed up that day. I made it through round after round of callbacks. Eight callbacks later, auditions concluded and we were told the nineteen people to be cast could expect a call "soon." That 212 number was my call.

Inside the too-quiet gift shop, near a large rack of Statue of Liberty snow globes, I stifled a scream as the casting director told me the exciting news: I was being offered a role to dance and sing in the ensemble and to understudy Glinda! Some people dream of being a CEO, others dream of being astronauts . . . I would be living a different kind of dream, playing a flying monkey, Ozian citizen, and the Mayoress of Munchkinland (complete with a white wig that resembled Martha Washington's updo). The tour would embark in a few months and play in theaters across the USA and nearly every Canadian province.

While any aspiring actor would be overjoyed, that call meant *everything* to me. It was as if the theater gods had seen my sacrifices and answered my prayers. Not that I really believed in "theater gods," of course. At that time if you had asked me who God was, I'd point to the *Catechism of the Catholic Church* and say I believed every word. However, the way I *lived* reflected a very different reality: theater sat squarely on the throne in my heart. The roles I booked and the skills I gained were the very definition of my self-worth.

My flawed beliefs certainly weren't a reflection of my upbringing. I grew up in a devout Catholic family. My parents raised eight children, of whom I am second oldest, and homes-chooled us way before homeschooling was trendy—we moved frequently because of my dad's military career. So, our social circle was centered in parish life, and I had many witnesses of faith around me. I have fond memories of volunteering with the Legion of Mary, celebrating at All Saints' Day parties with our homeschool groups, hosting our parish priests for dinner, and even having epic water-balloon fights with them on several occasions! As a child, I had a sincere love for God and found a spiritual mentor in St. Thérèse's *Story of a Soul*.

My childhood was simple, beautiful, and filled with faith. My parents took their duty to educate us seriously. We memorized sections of the *Catechism*, prayed a daily family rosary, read about the saint of the day, and even observed liturgical feast days with celebratory tea parties featuring themed food. I once built a convincing Lourdes "grotto" from Rice Krispies Treats. (Feel free to be envious.)

And yet, despite all that catechesis . . .

Somehow, *somehow* there was a crucial gap. Somehow, I missed the lesson that God is really interested in *me*. I thought he wanted the most demure, reverent Sunday version of me, not *also* my messiest, dorkiest side. I didn't know what to do with the negative emotions of shame, vengefulness, envy, and anger that arose in some of my relationships. Because they were undesirable and uncomfortable—the farthest thing from heav-enly—I assumed God was ashamed of them, too, so I pretended they didn't exist when I prayed. I had no idea that any time I turned my heart to him, even with half-formed thoughts, his heart swelled with delight and joy. I had no idea that he's on fire with the desire to speak to me, if I would just learn how to listen.

I never believed in my heart of hearts that he wants what's best for me *even more* than I want it.

I thought that, when he died on the Cross, it was for humanity en masse. I didn't realize it was for me, Stacey—*me particularly*.

Consequently, my prayer life looked something like this:

Hello, God. Thanks for being great and all.

Listen, I really want this thing. Could you please give it to me?

I really want it. If you don't want it for me, could you please change your mind?

I'm sure it'll be the best thing for me because I really want it.

Thanks. Bye.

And the quiet part that I wouldn't say aloud to him or even to myself: *If you don't give it to me, you're not really that good.* I didn't trust he knew what was best. If I'm totally honest, I wanted all the control in the relationship. A fearful part of me was sure his will would be exactly the thing that I hated, and so God never got authentic Stacey.

And because I didn't trust him, he wasn't firmly seated on the throne of my heart. In fact, the more I pursued my theater dreams, the more I relegated him to the little Sunday-morning corner of my week (and even then, I was often late because I was prioritizing my daily two-hour workout). I had yet to learn the lesson that I could do *all the religious things* and yet still not really be a Christian. I was comfortable treating God as my consultant or assistant rather than my Savior and Redeemer.

KEEPING UP APPEARANCES

It turns out, theater gods are cruel masters. The product I was selling at every audition was *me*, so I had better look my best and most appealing. I was extremely fit, but a hypoactive thyroid caused me always to sit at the top of what doctors would point to as a healthy BMI for my height. Since childhood the voices in my head had whispered accusingly that no one would love me unless I was thin. I wanted to be loved more than anything else. So, when the choreographer of a well-respected theater company told me I was "too big" to be considered for a role in their show, I caved. I went on a crash diet and discovered I could power walk two hours a day after eating nothing but Light + Fit yogurt and Fiber One granola bars.

Two weeks after the crash diet began, I came back to the choreographer fourteen pounds lighter. I had lost a pound a day, and I was faint with exhaustion. The choreographer was pleased, and I got the role I wanted. My classmates all noticed, and suddenly my senior year, I was *hot* stuff. The choreographer sent other girls to me for my diet plan. I got called in for auditions and booked roles at the top theaters in DC. I was the envy of all the girls in my college class (if there was a patron saint of the musical-theater program, it would be Our Lady of Perpetual Dieting!). I was finally, *finally* good enough.

The problem was, I was now locked into maintaining a size double-zero body, or all my new-found success would slip away. Sure, my parents and friends were worried about me, but what did that matter compared to the success I was finding? Every day, the scale dictated whether I was going to have a good day. If I had gained an ounce, I would whisper to myself, *You're stupid, fat, and ugly, and no one is ever going to love you.* Then I would work out even more, punishing myself.

And so, when at last I received that long-awaited phone call inviting me on tour, I knew I was about to embark on a great adventure, performing with that tour group. I had no idea I was about to discover something even better: a love letter written thousands of years ago.

DISCOVERING GOD ON THE YELLOW BRICK ROAD

The touring cast of *The Wizard of Oz* set off on a whirlwind of one-nighters (a different city each night). We played both glamorous historic Vaudeville houses with legendary actors' autographs scrawled across the walls, and ice-hockey rinks in rural Canada with boards laid down over the ice as a makeshift stage. We even played Harry Houdini's theater in Macon, Georgia, complete with Houdini's still-working trap door and a host of eerie stories of a resident ghost!

Happily, most of my castmates were relaxed people who saved drama for the stage. I particularly clicked with one bubbly young woman named Ana, who also played a Munchkin in the "Lullaby League." Ana's optimistic personality drew me, and our friendship deepened over our months of touring. She had a strong faith in God and attended Mass with me on Sundays.

It turns out, Ana also read the Bible. She could even quote it! This was entirely new to me for a Catholic. I knew that, if you attend daily Mass, you'll hear most of the Bible every three years, so I thought I was all set when it came to scripture. I had received a Bible for Confirmation that was collecting dust on my shelf at home. I hadn't even brought it with me to college.

Ana introduced me to reading scripture as a way to hear God speak to me. She jokingly called her habit of breaking open God's Word "churching," and I, fascinated, began to join her. We'd read a passage and discuss it in the hotel after the show. I had no idea what I was doing, but I felt as if I had discovered a treasure. *Why did no one ever show me how to do this before?* I wondered. I learned that even a tiny passage from scripture, even just one verse or one word, could contain enough spiritual fodder for a full meditation.

DIGEST SCRIPTURE DAILY

Slowly, scripture began to live in my heart. Years later I'd interview a scripture scholar named Joshua Mazrin, who told me that, just as our bodies digest a meal and it becomes a part of us, we're meant to "chew" or "digest" the Word of God. I didn't know it at the time, but that's what I was doing. Often, after an evening of "churching" with Ana, the next day I'd want to recall the exact words we had read. Some part of me realized those words had power. So, I'd read the verse again and underline it. I'd commit small verses to memory. Years later, those same verses still float to mind when I need them, especially in difficult times.

I didn't know it, but reading scripture was the beginning of hearing God speak to me. Ana was much further along at it than I was, so it seemed to come naturally to her. She digested what we read in light of a rich relationship of trust with God. For me, I felt as if I was a child discovering the stories of my mother's life before I was born. Babies think of themselves as the center of their parents' world, and they can't conceive that their parents had an entire set of experiences before they existed. I had glossed over so many Bible stories. Now I was entering in. *God, you did all this before I ever got here?* It was entrancing to focus on something—really, some*one*—besides my self-critical voices.

As I read, I marveled over the provision and the faithfulness of God to the Israelites, despite their fickle hearts. The cries of King David's heart in the Psalms—the highs and lows and everything in between—became my heart's cries to God.

Later, exploring the epistles of the New Testament, I began to claim as my personal mantra St. Paul's rallying words to the early Christians: "Live in a manner worthy of the calling you have received" (Ephesians 4:1). I began to seek enlightenment for the parts that were difficult to understand: *Why did the translator choose that strange word? What did these words of Christ mean to the Jews in his day? Why does Job start talking about ostriches?* (See Job 30:29. I still don't understand that one, to be honest.)

Ana's friendship was a gift from God, and I needed it. My self-abusive habits of undereating and overexercising were being shaken out of me. I had no control over my schedule or where our bus stopped for lunch breaks. If you've ever driven across the USA, you know that rural states don't offer much that's not fried and covered in cheese! Not only that, but bus calls before dawn often left no time to fit in my two-hour workouts.

My anxiety rose as the number on the scale began to climb. My sense of control—a prison I had willingly inhabited for years—was being eroded. After years of entrapment, those bars felt safe. I just didn't know how to live without my false beliefs.

My anxiety came to a head one day on our lunch break from the bus. I had eaten "too much" (by my ridiculous standards) free hotel breakfast that morning, and I had spent the morning wallowing in shame. I was sick of the voices telling me I wasn't good enough and wasn't lovable, but I didn't know how to let go. I just wished I could be perfect without having to sacrifice every ounce of my mental and physical energy. I wandered listlessly through the mall, a litany of self-defeat ringing in my head. *I wish I could get a burger. Too greasy. I should probably eat something because I have to perform tonight. There's a salad place, but I have salad every day. Nothing I can eat sounds good. Never mind. I've gone days without eating before, and I can do it again. I hate living like this.*

Ana spent the lunch break with me, listening patiently to my complaints, and we got back on the bus without my having eaten anything. About an hour later, she came to my seat and tapped me on the shoulder. "Stacey, sometimes the Holy Spirit gives me verses for people, and I think he gave me this one for you." She opened her Bible and pointed to Song of Songs 4:9: "You have stolen my heart, my sister, my bride, with one glance of your eyes, with one jewel of your necklace."

Have you ever looked at the sky as the sun cast its rays through a cloud? Those words were like light breaking through the clouds in my heart. Something massive clicked internally. I felt as if I had been invited up a mountain to look down on myself, and what I saw took my breath away. God's view of me my entire life was entirely different than mine. What he saw was captivating and thoroughly beautiful—so beautiful that I had stolen his heart with just a glance his way.

In fact, I am—we all are—so beautiful because I look like him. In Genesis we read, "In his image he created them." God by his nature is goodness, truth, beauty, and love. For the first time I realized, *I look like love.* And then I realized, *I always have . . . and I don't have to do anything to earn it.* I felt my soul take a massive breath. *I'm not just okay, acceptable, fine . . . I'm beloved without having to do anything about it. And I always have been.* I finally saw what was waiting for me beyond the bars of my self-criticism: a freedom of existence I had forgotten years ago.

MAKING GOD'S BELIEFS MINE

I rode on a spiritual high for weeks after Ana told me the life-changing Song of Songs verse, feeling integrated for the first time in years. That feeling subsided eventually, as any high does. Eventually, the devil began whispering the old lies, and I had to combat them daily, sometimes hourly, sometimes minute to minute, with scripture. A famous study by the National Science Foundation found that the average person has between 12,000 and 60,000 thoughts per day. About 95 percent of them are recycled, and 80 percent of them are negative. I wasn't alone in my tendency toward negative thinking. That's an enormous number of thoughts to wrest away from the devil and transform toward God's thinking.

I began to understand that God's voice has a "tone" to it. His voice challenges and invites but never accuses. Pope Francis expressed it beautifully in a mini-lesson on discernment and hearing the voice of God during his May 3, 2020 *Regina Caeli* address: "God *proposes* himself, He does not *impose* himself. . . . The voice of God, instead, corrects us, with great patience, but always encourages us, consoles us: it always nourishes hope. God's voice is a voice that has a horizon, whereas the voice of the evil one leads you to a wall, it backs you into a corner." Lo and behold, the accusatory voice that kept me on a literal and figurative treadmill of self-hatred was never God's; it was the enemy in disguise!

The devil likes to use circumstances—an audition where I didn't get a callback, for example—and twist them into shameful thoughts. His intent is to back you into a corner, while God's intent is to invite you forward in hope. As I was discovering my new love for reading scripture, a friend gave me the book *My Stroke of Insight* by Jill Bolte Taylor. Jill, a neuroscientist, explains to nonscientists like me that our brains run in circuits. Ever heard the expression "train of thought"? It's pretty accurate; our thought circuits are similar to a train running on a circular track. The more often you consent to hop on the train, the stronger the circuit grows and the more it becomes your default thought.

As an example, I felt the devil suggesting the thought, "You didn't get a callback because you're not talented and no one likes to watch you perform." The negative, self-critical train of thought had become so habitual that I defaulted to that. I'd walk around blaming myself instead and fixate on my imperfections rather than showing myself compassion, allowing for the endless possibilities of why I didn't get the callback. Maybe my voice wasn't the right one for the role. Maybe someone else looked the part more than I did. Maybe the casting director already had the role cast in his mind before auditions even began.

Jill's book not only illuminated brain science but also presented the solution to retraining your brain so it no longer defaults to untrue, self-critical trains of thought. I adapted her method using scripture. I began to notice that when my thoughts changed, my actions followed suit. When I understood that I was God's beloved daughter, I began to act like one. A daughter of God wouldn't abuse her body; she would honor it for the gift and miracle it is.

When something undesirable happened and I felt a negative train of thought pulling up to the figurative station in my mind, I'd press an imaginary "pause" button in my head. I recognized that I couldn't stay off the train of my own volition because I was addicted. So, I'd hand the negative lie up to God and ask him to take it away. He came to my aid every single time. The lies would dissipate instantly, and my mind would be free! The final step was to thank God and recall his words from scripture. I began to memorize snippets of scripture in my daily reading and recite them to myself to fill the empty space in my mind.

I had to do this hour to hour, and sometimes minute to minute, for several weeks before I began to see real results. Surrendering my thoughts and achieving freedom felt great and built a bridge of trust with the Lord. Within six months, the years of negative thought circuits were broken and were no longer my default. I still think self-critical thoughts, but now I have the freedom to examine them dispassionately and reject them if they're undeserved.

This method worked great, provided I followed it diligently. I had to develop a daily "battle plan" of reading and digesting scripture. I wrote down God's life-giving words in my journal, on my hand, on a sticky note on the mirror—wherever I would see them. Even if I didn't receive a life-changing word or phrase as I prayed each day, I learned that I always felt peace afterward. I began to learn God's generosity: for a small investment of my time, he blessed my day with joy. I felt as if I could ask him for things, and that it wasn't annoying to him; rather, he *wanted* me to! When I read verses such as, "For the Lord delights in you, and will claim you as his bride" (Isaiah 62:4), it felt as though they were written directly to me.

ENDURING TRIALS USING SCRIPTURE

Every Christian experiences periods of consolation (feeling close to God and being excited to pray) and desolation (feeling far from God and dryness in prayer). Intense desolation can result from hard circumstances, and in those times I'm always grateful to find God's promises and help in his words in scripture.

For example, there was a time I wrote in my journal about feeling abandoned and separated from God, as though he had turned his face from me. A four-month trial of desolation in prayer was stretching out with no end in sight. The length of my trial terribly tested my belief in God's love for me. I thought, *God, how can I trust you if you are turning your face from me? Show me the truth . . . Are you still there for me?*

I showed up with questions and found answers soon after, as I continued my daily practice of reading the Bible (I'll describe my routine later in this chapter). One day I was reading 1 Chronicles and happened across the verse, "Rely on the might Lord; constantly seek his face" (16:11). Another day, I was reading the book of Job and found another piece of my "peace puzzle," when Job describes God's consoling presence in the aftermath of his losses: "By hearsay I have heard of you, but now *my eye has seen you*" (emphasis mine). And in the Psalms, I read, "The Lord is just and loves just deeds; *the upright will see his face*" (11:7, emphasis mine). The Lord was gently telling me he's not hiding from me but is doing deep work I can't understand yet. He wants me, and he'll never stop loving me. As circumstances unfolded, I came to understand that the trial that felt never-ending was indeed sent to strengthen and purify me.

Instances like this happen many, many times. Each instance feels like a small miracle. I just need to make efforts to meet God daily by reading his words and digesting what I've read.

MAKE READING GOD'S WORD A HABIT

As time has gone on, I've developed a simple structure that's doable even on the busiest days. The beauty of this method is that reading scripture never gets too dry (trust me, we all lose steam in the rules and rubrics of Leviticus!). Here's what I do:

- I read four chapters of scripture daily: two chapters of the Old Testament (starting from Genesis), one of the Psalms, and one chapter of the New Testament (starting from Matthew). By reading chronologically in three different places, I get the full picture of salvation history. When the Old Testament feels dry, the Psalms are evocative and emotional. The New Testament reveals the lives and teachings of Jesus and the apostles that help me follow Jesus. Even reading slowly, reading four chapters takes ten to fifteen minutes.
- As I read, I pay attention to what strikes me as strange, what I don't understand, or which words hit my heart as a personal answer or love note from the Lord. I underline and date them in my Bible, or write about them in my journal. Sometimes I just take a mental note and know I'll return to those words. But the physical activity of underlining and marking helps me to process what I read.
- Finally, I spend about ten minutes praying about what I just read. I think about the words that stood out, and I ask the Holy Spirit for understanding. If I read a story, I imagine putting myself in the scene. Sometimes I feel God beginning

to direct the conversation with images or words. (This was difficult to trust at first and still doesn't happen every day.) When I feel distracted, I just keep coming back to the words.

God used the most unlikely circumstances—meeting a Munchkin on a Broadway National Tour—to teach me how to connect with him. As I slowly learned to claim my freedom and converse with God through scripture, I was a very long way from surrender. I still wanted to sit in the driver's seat of my future. But the fire had been lit in my heart, and the adventure was beginning.

YOUR ADVENTURE AWAITS: JOURNAL PROMPTS

God has an adventure waiting for you! It's an adventure as unique as you are: your desires, your gifts, and your strengths and abilities. Above all, it's an adventure in which God will teach you to surrender your heart completely and to discover for yourself the divine intimacy for which you were created.

Your adventure will look very different from mine—and yet I hope that you will benefit from the lessons I learned about how to hear God's voice and discern his will. As I share my own story, I pray that it will help you to recognize similar movements and moments in your own life. Here are a few journal prompts to get you started—you'll find similar prompts and exercises at the end of each chapter.

Can you recall a time when God seemed to speak to you through scripture, perhaps when you were either hearing it at Mass or reading it on your own?

🏔 What are some untruths about yourself or God that have created distance between you and God? Ask God to open your eyes to the truth. Find a verse you can commit to memory to help you.

🏔 Do you have a regular practice of reading the Bible and other spiritual reading? If not, where can you carve out fifteen minutes in your day regularly to make it happen?

🏔 Who are some of the people God has brought into your life to teach you what it means to follow Jesus? What are some of the most important things you learned?

2

ONIONS AND WORMS

HOW GOD SPEAKS THROUGH OUR DESIRES AND DISCONTENTMENT

Find your delight in the Lord who will give
you your heart's desire.

—Psalm 37:4

After *The Wizard of Oz* tour ended, I moved to New York, ready to take Broadway by storm. I was twenty-two, (overly) ambitious, and energetic; with a National Tour credit on my resume, the world was my oyster. *Now my real life can start*, I thought. I scored an amazing studio apartment two blocks from Central Park, on 56th Street nestled between Eighth and Ninth Avenues. It was only about five hundred square feet, but by NYC standards it was amazing!

Within a few months I had established my usual haunts: the tapas restaurant where I worked, my favorite delis and frozen-yogurt spots, my dance studio and parish, and the audition studios where I walked each day to hammer away at my dream. I quickly fell in with a group of young adults at my parish and was invited to the leadership team. I remember being impressed that the group was so well organized and active in its outreach to the community.

I had incredible enthusiasm for my faith after developing a scripture-reading habit on tour; at that time in my life, God was affirming in me his loving, irrevocable parenthood. As I lifted my heart to him in many little moments throughout my day, he slowly rewired my brain's false paradigms to reflect the truth of my inherent dignity. I wanted to tell everyone about the transformation God was working in me.

Church became a crucial part of my social circle; I could organize a group dinner or an ice-cream social or a Gifts of the Holy Spirit–themed mixer with the best of 'em. I'd often invite other actors at auditions to church with me if spirituality came up in our conversations. My friend group avoided the "big no's"—drugs, sex, and excessive alcohol. For the first time in a long time, I felt like a "real" Catholic. *Look at me, Mom, doing all the Catholic things in the middle of NYC! Aren't you proud?*

The thing was, I was doing a lot of good things, but my relationship with God needed to go deeper. I was still comfortable in my worldliness, though by all appearances my faith was thriving. For example, hearing at Mass the parable of the servant who hid his talents, I immediately used it to justify my career choices. *I'm not like that guy, letting my talents go to waste—I'm going for my dreams as hard as I can!* I took a single scripture passage and used it to justify everything I wanted.

God still had too little influence on my will and my choices. If he asked me to do something I didn't want to do, I ignored or resisted him. I didn't want to put him in the driver's seat of my life—the one thing he really wanted me to do. This became clear to me about the same time I booked my second National Tour, *Beauty and the Beast*. For eleven months I played Marie, the Baker's wife. In the opening number, the Baker says, "Marie! The baguettes! Hurry up!" That was my cue to scurry stage left to stage right, carrying those baguettes. *What a noble contribution to humanity*, right? I also understudied Mrs. Potts and the Wardrobe and played a fork, a plate, and a napkin.

It was during this time that I watched my life plan unravel. We traveled with few opportunities to see anyone outside our dysfunctional "tour family." One day it was Bozeman, Montana; then Boise, Idaho; after that a border crossing to some city named Kamloops in British Columbia, Canada. We rode the bus up to twelve hours a day. The daily gossip, broken confidences, and bickering became intolerable. I went by myself to Mass every week, sharing as little as possible of myself with anyone—except for the occasional flashes of un-Christian anger. As we glittered and flashed our way through "Be Our Guest," I could feel tears streaming down my face behind my false lashes and lipstick-laden smile.

I must have looked absolutely ridiculous: a dancing fork wearing a gold leotard and LaDuca heels, sobbing her eyes out. I knew it, but the stage was the only place I felt safe to let my feelings out. I was lonely. I missed being proud of myself and my work, and I missed my family and my Catholic friends. In this toxic environment, my thought life deteriorated and I lost my drive to audition for future shows. A little voice whispered,

This isn't it. You're drifting farther and farther from the person you want to be.

I didn't realize it at first, but God was speaking to me through this little gut instinct, this worm of discontent. Time taught me that that little voice is never wrong. It can tell you a relationship has passed its expiration date, a job isn't the right fit for you, or you're deceiving yourself.

I tried hard to ignore the voice, but I couldn't kick it. Even worse, I couldn't shake the big question this voice forced me to ask: *If I don't want to be a Broadway performer anymore, what do I want?* Instead of feeling more fulfilled by living my dream, I felt empty. I had no idea what a gift that emptiness would prove to be.

Right away I knew I wasn't just dealing with a case of stage fright, which typically resolves itself with an endorphin rush when the performance begins. The "worm of discontent" was quieter. It was a heaviness in the pit of my stomach that spoke when I was alone. I tried to distract myself and ignore it. I didn't realize it at the time, but I was better off tuning into it. It was both massively inconvenient *and* the key to my happiness.

DESIRE THE RIGHT END

The worm of discontent is a gift; it awakens us to the fact that we're trying to expand a finite goal to make it fill an infinite space in our hearts. St. Thomas Aquinas taught that we have two kinds of desires: desires of means (which are finite and oriented toward achieving an end or goal) and desires of ends (which are infinite and grow according to our understanding).

For example, a desire for physical fitness could be pursued as an end in itself (a desire of means)—in order to achieve a two-hour workout. In this scenario, with my end goal being the maximum amount of fitness possible, I would desire an infinite level of fitness. Very often that desire involves unhealthy choices, such as working myself to exhaustion, poor eating habits, and turning my mirror and scale into gods that dictate every choice of my empty life.

In an ideal scenario that aligns with my faith on the other hand, pursuing fitness and a healthy body would be a desire of means, while my end desire would be to serve the Lord and carry out his will. Having a healthy body would be a *means* to carrying out the *end* goal of fulfilling God's mission. In that scenario, I only want as much fitness and health as I need to pursue my bigger goal. Therefore, my desire for fitness (my desire of means) is finite, while pursuing God's will (my desire of ends) is infinite. In this scenario I aim for three or four thirty-minute workouts per week, and if a family or friend needs me during my scheduled workout times, they are the higher priority.

What makes a desire healthy or unhealthy is not simply the object of our desire, but what motivates us to pursue it. We will never be satisfied so long as we make anything other than God our highest priority. Only God is infinite, and in the words of St. Augustine in his *Confessions*, "Our hearts are restless until they rest in you, O Lord."

At that time in my life, I was still in the early stages of my Christian walk, and Broadway was the biggest dream I could imagine. Even so, the worm of discontent reminded me over and over that my dream still wasn't big enough. In the words of C. S. Lewis, "It would seem that . . . our desires [are] not too strong, but too weak. We are half-hearted creatures, fooling about with

drink and sex and ambition when infinite joy is offered us. [We
are] like an ignorant child who wants to go on making mud pies
in a slum because he cannot imagine what is meant by the offer
of a holiday at the sea. We are far too easily pleased."[1] I had been
trying to make my Broadway dream my desire of ends, but the
Lord himself was awakening me, through my discontent, to the
reality that only he can be my end desire.

Looking back on the times I felt disillusioned and empty on
tour, now I see what a blessing the emptiness was. To receive
the great gifts God wanted to give me, he needed me to pry my
clenched fists open and drop the dream that couldn't fulfill me.
Only when I felt the emptiness, the lack, and my own inability
to control my own happiness could I turn to him and let him
fill me.

YOU ARE AN ONION

Remember that scene in the movie *Shrek* where the ogre, Shrek,
is trying to explain his desires to Donkey? As they walk through
a field, he cracks an onion in half to show that "ogres are like
onions" because they have layers. Do me a favor and think of
yourself as an onion for a minute. (Very flattering, I know.)

My outer layer—that is, my most surface-level desire at any
given moment—is for *necessities*: breathing, eating, and sleeping.

The layer under that is *comfort*: fuzzy socks for my icy feet,
mint Oreo milkshakes on a hot day, kicking back with a glass of
red wine and a movie in the evening. But even if those desires
are gratified, I won't be fulfilled—at least, not for long. Lying on
the beach would get boring after a week or so, and bingeing on
Netflix every night would leave me feeling a sense of "ick."

Ultimately, I know I wasn't made just for comfort. I need *purpose*. Purpose is the next layer of the onion. Looking back over my journals from my teenage years, I can see the common threads in my desires. It astounds me that, while I've lived out my desires differently in different seasons, *my deep desires have never changed.* I wanted to be a part of something bigger than myself and to live in community. I wanted to connect deeply with others and to discover all that is truly good and beautiful. I wanted the transcendent . . . and my worm of discontent would never let me settle for the lights on Broadway. I wanted more. And God wanted more for me. Much more.

Now, there was a time when I thought my Broadway desires were the deepest layer. I thought they were, I wanted them to be, and I built my identity and my life on them for nine years. I wanted human validation—but that desire was improperly ordered; I thought it was a desire of ends when it should have been a desire of means (a means to draw me to the love and validation I truly needed—which only God can provide).

Of course, I had noble desires mixed in with my Broadway dreams too. I loved collaborating with others to create something bigger than any of us. I loved connecting deeply with my castmates and the audience, and presenting truths that would lift them up and inspire them. Those noble desires were pointing me toward the next right step.

FIXED VERSUS GROWTH MINDSETS

At first I was reluctant to give up my Broadway dream. *Wouldn't it be like admitting I had wasted those years? Wouldn't I look flaky to all my friends and family? And how would I find my new sense of purpose?*

In my *Called and Caffeinated* podcast interview with January Donovan, we talked about fixed versus growth mindsets. A fixed mindset keeps us trapped: I *have* to be this kind of person, I *have* to do this thing, I *have* to appear this way to these people, I *have* to be in this place, and so on. With a fixed mindset, you're tethered to an idea of yourself. Think of the flash-in-the-pan celebrities: they put out one great film or album, then fade.

People who remain successful through changes and seasons have a growth mindset. With a growth mindset, you're free to set your sights higher and higher. You're a student of life, constantly learning and dreaming bigger. You are adaptable and can pivot when needed. You need humility to live this way, seeing yourself as the work in progress you are. Let's be honest: no one has it figured out. There is no giant answer sheet in the sky telling us what our futures hold.

The devil is on Team Fixed Mindset. As I knew from my eating disorder, he loves to twist the truth and use it to back you into a corner. He concocts negative, accusatory voices and unattainable expectations to keep you trapped. And worst of all, he tells you it's God's voice.

God, on the other hand, is on Team Growth Mindset. He's always loving, always ready to forgive, always ready to expand your vision of yourself. He sees the great potentiality for which you were created.

For months, my fixed mindset of myself as an actor destroyed my happiness and caused massive anxiety. I lived reactively, afraid to step into the unknown. I was scared that, if I followed God's will, I'd have to deny all my desires and sign up for something I didn't want. I worried I would feel *less* myself the holier I became, and so I was scared to become holy.

Nothing could be further from the truth. In more than eighty episodes of the *Called and Caffeinated* podcast, my guests have reiterated the same truth, time and again: when God calls us to holiness, he is calling us to be *more* ourselves. Your desires and God's desires for you aren't opposed to each other; rather, at the deepest level (the core of the onion, so to speak), they are *one and the same*. When you ask God to sit in the driver's seat, you're simultaneously discerning what *you* want most.

Stop for a minute and let that sink in.

God doesn't want to frustrate your desires: he wants to fulfill them. Do you believe that? Or are you afraid to hear God's voice calling you to his plan? If you believe it intellectually, do you *act* as though you believe it, consulting God about your plans daily in prayer and listening for his answer?

When I quit theater, I didn't do these things. And yet, as I continued reading scripture, God persisted in speaking to my heart as a child of the King, heiress of the kingdom of God. Could a princess of the kingdom be satisfied with worldly fame? Absolutely not! I was made for far more than that!

Enter the worm of discontent to awaken her more noble, deeper desires . . .

EXPAND YOUR DESIRES

In his *Spiritual Exercises*, St. Ignatius of Loyola offers us a time-honored course for understanding God's purpose for us. He says, "Man is created to praise, reverence, and serve God our Lord, and by this means to save his soul. And the other things on the face of the earth are created for man and that they may help him in prosecuting the end for which he is created. From this it follows that man is to use them as much as they help him on to his end, and ought to rid himself of them so far as they hinder him as to it."[2]

St. Ignatius continues, "In every good election [meaning decision], as far as depends on us, the eye of our intention ought to be simple, only looking at what we are created for, namely, the praise of God our Lord and the salvation of our soul. And so, I ought to choose whatever I do, that it may help me for the end for which I am created, not ordering or bringing the end to the means, but the means to the end."[3]

Essentially, he's writing that the purpose of *every single thing* in this life is to help us attain heaven, and if it's not helping us attain heaven, then we should detach ourselves from it. Union with God in heaven is the biggest dream possible, and that's the end or goal to which our current desires, no matter how noble or otherwise, are pointing us.

The end St. Ignatius refers to is the eternal salvation of your soul. So every temporal choice, says St. Ignatius, is well ordered when your priorities are directed toward eternity. You owe it to God, to yourself, and to the people you're called to serve to think about the end, the purpose, of your life. The micro should serve the macro.

My Broadway dream wasn't my deepest dream, but only by pursuing it could I get to the next layer. I had to walk through each audition and show, gain resilience and skills along the way, experience failure, and learn about my desires to get to the next step. Acting on my dream taught me that I couldn't make myself happy. Soon I'd discover that following God's will would make me feel more myself, more motivated, more excited, and more

alive. There is nothing better than learning to live for your purpose rather than yourself.

DARE TO MAKE A CHANGE

For me, the next layer of my desire revealed itself slowly, with
no grand plan. I love checking off a to-do list, but now I had to
learn to be led and to listen. I continued my day job as a wait-
ress but stopped going to auditions. Instead of getting in line
with the other Broadway hopefuls every morning, I prioritized
receiving Our Lord in Holy Communion at daily Mass. I was
finally returning the dedicated gaze he had given me my whole
life. Although I felt like a total mess externally, I felt peace when
I prayed. I ended an unhealthy relationship that had passed its
expiration date. Knowing God was there for me gave me courage
to face my fear of being alone. I began to find new friends who
spoke a common language with me of seeking God's will more
deeply. For the first time, I dared to ask, "God, what do you want
for my life?"

Moving away from something you know is wrong for you is
scary, especially when you don't yet know what to move toward.
Below are some journaling prompts to help you clarify your
desires and resolve the conflicting voices. After journaling and
praying, make a concrete resolution to make the change(s) you
know you need. It's hard, but you're not alone.

YOUR ADVENTURE AWAITS: JOURNAL PROMPTS

Here are a few journal prompts for you to consider any worm of discontent in your life and whether you need to make a change.

- Do you believe God is speaking to you through the desires he has placed on your heart? Why or why not?

- Do you feel the worm of discontent in your life in any of the following areas: a friendship, relationship, job, living situation, something else? What is the worm urging you to do?

- What are you afraid you might lose if you make a change? (Identify it; don't judge!) Invite God into your journaling, then imagine with him what your life could be. Don't censor or judge anything. Imagine the highest highs you can think of!

- Are you under the influence of negative, accusatory voices that are keeping you in a fixed mindset? What do they say, and how do they "sound"? What is one thing you can do right now to move toward a growth mindset?

Look at what you just wrote. Ask for God's help discerning how to respond to the challenges you are facing. If it entails something you feel unable to control—either because you lack the strength or for some other reason—and it is endangering your soul, let go of it. If this challenge is something you can correct, identify one concrete thing you can do immediately to make a positive change.

3

JUST DO IT?

HOW GOD SPEAKS THROUGH OUR CHOICES AND ACTIONS

When you call me, and come and pray to me,
I will listen to you. When you look for me, you
will find me. Yes, when you seek me with all
your heart, I will let you find me.
—Jeremiah 29:13–14

"Thanks for your time, Stacey! We'll be in touch!" The screen went blank as the casting agent ended the video call.

"Well, that was hilarious," I said aloud to myself. Just as I was giving up my quest for public appearances, a TV production company asked me to chat.

It was an ordinary weekday. I ran to daily Mass that morning, and when I got back there was an email from a dear friend who

was pursuing a film career in Los Angeles. She had recommend-
ed me for an unspecified video project featuring Catholic young
women between the ages of twenty and thirty. The language was
vague, and the message contained an email address to contact.
Intrigued, I dashed off a few lines about myself and went about
my day.

An hour later, a casting agent called. He asked questions
about my faith life. I felt very relaxed; I had zero investment in
this project. What even was the project? No one knew at that
point, as it was in the early stages of development. The agent
seemed pleased and asked to video chat. We did, then I heard
nothing for a month.

As the days elapsed, the questions about my future continued
to swirl. I was slowing down and noticing a different side of life.
I was prioritizing daily Mass, even if it meant skipping auditions.
A few weeks after my *Beauty and the Beast* tour ended, I signed
up for a week of service with a missionary group in the Bronx.
A year before I would have been anxious to leave the audition
scene for a week, even to go on vacation! Now I was going to stay
in a house with women I'd never met, doing whatever they told
me to do for a week, totally unconcerned about the auditions I
was missing.

While I was away, a casting agent called me for a cruise-ship
gig for which I'd auditioned months before. I turned it down,
choosing instead to spend more time ministering to people in
homeless shelters and gathering in communal prayer. The sur-
roundings were humble, but there was a depth and beauty that
made the most glamorous Broadway opening-night party feel
cheap.

One of the missionaries on my team was discerning a call to
religious life with the Franciscan Friars of the Renewal. I asked

him lots of questions, and I'll never forget the peace and joy in his eyes. They were windows to a soul in love with God. (A year later I ran into him at a holy hour run by the friars. He was in his year of postulancy and looked happier than ever!)

That week of service was a real wake-up call for me. In all the years I'd dedicated to theater, I had convinced myself that my art was my contribution to the world. I suddenly became aware that giving my time to others *in the ways they needed* was a more authentic contribution. I was surprised by how good and right it felt to love others that way. The sacrifice of my time was nothing compared to the gratification I felt from seeing the effects of my effort. It felt like coming home to myself.

Although the week of service didn't produce answers about my "big plan," it was an action step God could work with. I wasn't just praying: I was in motion, and now I'd had a taste of his peace. Because our ultimate call is self-donation, every selfless thing we do helps reveal our path. Service teaches me about myself, makes me more grateful, and connects me with incredible people who inadvertently lead me to the next right thing. I didn't plan that going into the week of service, of course, but it just happened that way. I think God likes to prove he can't be outdone in generosity: When we give him a day, he gives us a month of peace. When we give him a year to discern his will, he gives us a lifetime of purpose and happiness. And when we give him our whole life, he gives us eternity.

A few weeks later that summer, my mom gave me a book called *The Ear of the Heart*, the biography of Dolores Hart, an actress who famously became Elvis's first on-screen movie kiss. Dolores enjoyed success in many Hollywood movies and on Broadway in the 1950s. Then, at age twenty-four and at the height of her career, she broke off an engagement and left acting to become a cloistered Dominican nun in Bethlehem, Connecticut.

As I read Mother Dolores's story, I felt a lump rising in my throat and my heart thumping loudly. Her interior and exterior journey resonated deeply with me. *No way. No way, God. I don't want to be a nun. Please don't call me to be a nun. I still love ballet and singing show tunes! Dolores could give it all up because obviously it wasn't too important to her, but I need to live an artistic life to be fulfilled.*

DESIRES AND DISTRACTIONS

While all this was going on, one of my side hustles (I've had many!) was finding success. This side hustle takes a little explaining, so hang tight for a quick episode of *Weird Ways Stacey's Made a Living*.

It started at age six when my mom gave me Sculpey clay for Christmas. I loved it and sat for hours crafting up all kinds of miniature food, flowers, and knick-knacks. In tenth grade, my English teacher gave us an assignment I loved: try something new—anything—and write a paper about it. Well, I took my Sculpey clay and sculpted an eighteen-inch-high version of my teacher! It resembled him, right down to the tiny coke-bottle glasses and his signature gray vest I'd crafted from a sock. (I'm told he still pranks his classes by hiding in the closet and leaving the doll on his desk as their "substitute teacher.")

Years later, this funny little hobby of sculpting miniature people took off when my tour castmates requested sculptures of themselves in costume as mementos of their roles. It was the perfect way to pass time on our bus rides between cities, and it was fun to feel my castmates' anticipation of each new little work of art. Sculpting became my relaxing artistic haven, and requests were flowing in as friends showed friends their "mini-me's."

So, you've guessed by now I'm an artsy type, right? Dancing, singing, acting, sculpting? Such an artistic person could never be fulfilled as a nun, right? Sure, there was that year between ages eight and nine when I said I wanted to become a bride of Christ after leafing through my parents' coffee-table picture book on the life of St. Thérèse of Lisieux . . . but I also wanted to be a mom *and* an actress too! Anyway, who even knows anything at age eight? No, consecrated life definitely wasn't for me.

Yet, the suspicion kept nagging. It felt a lot like the worm of discontent, and I was pretty sick of that voice.

A few weeks later, as I jolted along in a squealing subway car, the TV production office called me back. The agent told me they had settled on a subject for the show about Catholic young women. And what was it? *Women discerning becoming nuns.* She asked if they could come to my apartment and interview me on camera.

I thought about all that had happened in the past few months, and I wondered if this was a sign. Was God calling me to be a nun? The thought scared me, but my intrigue was too great to refuse. I had a mysterious sense there was something waiting in it for me. I was honest with the agent: becoming a nun was far from the top of my list of desired paths. She assured me it was okay, as long as I was open to it and there were no impediments.

The camera crew arrived and asked me lots of questions. They seemed more intent on ensuring I was a "real" Catholic, and not just doing this interview to be on TV. *Trust me,* I thought. *If I wanted a career in film, I wouldn't be doing this today!* It all hit too close to home as I wrestled with my newfound lack of motivation for an acting career. My heart had learned to aspire to more. And it was uncomfortable with its newfound limitlessness. Just as Mother Dolores heard a call no one in Hollywood could understand, my heart was slowly learning to speak a new language.

I used to show up at auditions desperate to be liked. I'd wait for a call for hours, hoping I'd be one of the fortunate few asked in for final callbacks. This TV show interview was the absolute opposite. I felt totally comfortable, joking around with the camera men as if we were all just there to chill. Once again, after they left, I said, "Well, that was hilarious!" to myself. I didn't think about it, and I heard nothing more.

Shortly after that, I met a guy. He was a tall, Catholic, handsome musician visiting NYC who asked me on a proper date (a rare and precious thing for a woman in New York City!). He took his faith seriously. *This is great!* I thought. *I'm off the hook for religious life. Here's the guy. Sign me up!* The only problem was, I discovered within a few months that I didn't feel like myself around him. We dated long-distance, and each time we saw each other I cried my eyes out afterward. Our dates were punctuated by discomfort and insecurity. He didn't like my taste in music, was suspicious of my friend group, and questioned almost everything about me—including my taste in clothes! I felt as if I'd been judged and found wanting. Yet, we attended Mass together and had all the same values. I really wanted to make this work.

I was taking action to try and find my next step, but things felt messier and messier. I look back now and see all the threads woven together like a tapestry. I was zoomed in too close at the time to see the picture each thread made, but in hindsight it makes sense. There was a plan, and I just needed to keep taking action each day in the way I knew to be best in that moment. My best was good enough for God. He wasn't giving up on me; he was excited to unfold each step of the adventure for his dear girl. Action was purifying and clarifying my desires.

I met my boyfriend's mother and was completely befuddled as to why she didn't like me. People usually find me easy to get along with. Why did I feel like a disappointment to her? As I choked back tears on the train home, I thought of how the adults in my life had always told me my twenties were my best years. Yet here I was, feeling utterly directionless. I was too much and not enough. How would I even know when the right thing came along?

MY VISIT WITH MOTHER DOLORES

I kept leaning on my favorite verse: "For I know well the plans I have in mind for you—plans for your welfare and not for woe, so as to give you a future of hope" (Jeremiah 29:11). I didn't know how God was going to reveal his big plan for me—whatever that might be. My faith wavered many times, but I determinedly kept bringing my lonely heart back to him for answers.

A week later, the plot thickened. After six months of total silence, the production team informed me I was one of five young women selected to document my discernment journey on a Lifetime reality docuseries. We would visit convents and be followed by cameras. Mixed in with dread and horror was just enough fascination to *just not say no yet*. So, what did I do? I took action again: I impulsively drove to Bethlehem, Connecticut, to see Mother Dolores Hart.

I showed up at the Abbey of Regina Laudis totally unannounced, with no appointment. I don't know what I was thinking: maybe I assumed nuns sit around waiting for young women who could star in *Hot Mess: The Musical!* to show up for a visit? As I walked up the main driveway, I spied metal artwork dotting the grounds. *Did the nuns make those?* It wasn't my idea of how a cloistered nun would spend her time at all. I knocked at the door and the portress answered, an elderly nun with beautiful porcelain skin. Hardly able to breathe, I asked to see Mother Dolores.

The portress looked at me and said with a sigh of deepest disappointment, "You don't understand how the Abbey works at all." I gulped. She told me to wait at the door, then left. I fidgeted in the unseasonably warm February sunlight.

Fifteen minutes later, Mother Dolores Hart rounded the corner. Though the decades showed in her wrinkled skin, her blue eyes were still just as clear and piercing as in the beauty shots from her twenties. I charged forward, clasped her hands, and began telling her my story, hoping she could tell me what to do.

Mother Dolores listened patiently and asked a few questions. She cocked her head and inquired about my relationship and whether I felt peace. "Whoever he loves," she said, "it has to *be* you." In other words, it couldn't be a version of me that didn't really exist. My vocation would have to fit me like a glove. It would have to be something I wanted, not something I chose out of joyless obligation.

When I told her about the reality TV show, she gave a little smile. "Why not?" Her blue eyes danced playfully. I suddenly realized why I found it hard to say no: the show, and the real discernment of religious life itself, felt like an adventure. It was a risky one, in which I stood to lose every ounce of respect on worldwide TV. But still, a little *yes* popped into my heart. Mother

Dolores invited me to write to her. Before we parted, she said, "Maybe you should come back and audition for Annie. We're putting on *Annie Get Your Gun* this summer at our theater."

I'd forgotten that the nuns ran a summer theater on their property. I thanked Mother Dolores and wandered back out into the sunshine, taking in the metal sculptures and musing on what had passed between us. I stopped in at the gift shop where I saw the handmade cards and famous cheeses for sale—one cheese-making nun had even written a book! I stopped into the chapel to pray and witnessed the nuns chanting the Liturgy of the Hours. They sounded like angels, and I felt my soul breathe as I took in their beautiful tones. *These ladies find more ways to be artistic than I'd imagined*, I thought.

The greatest surprise still awaited me. The employee in the gift shop had urged me not to miss the crèche in the woods on my visit to the Abbey. I didn't know what could be so special about a crèche—wasn't it late February, well past the Christmas season? But since I'd come this far, I thought I might as well follow the signs pointing toward a patch of shady evergreens.

I followed the signs deeper into the pines to a little wooden hut. As I pushed open the door, it took my eyes a moment to adjust to the dim lights. I gasped. Spread out before my eyes were dozens and dozens of miniature people. *They look just like my Sculpey dolls!* They were posed, some closer and some farther from the Holy Family in the center. Some gazed at the Christ Child, transfixed. Others bickered among themselves. Still others busied themselves about their work, too swept up to notice the humble baby. I gaped in amazement. The signs indicated that the crèche was a duplicate of another set displayed in the Metropolitan Museum of Art. Both crèche were crafted in Italy in the

1600s. When the nuns acquired it, they carefully restored each figure, sewing new clothes or resculpting the figures.

I sat down weakly. I couldn't believe it. The ridiculous specificity of finding nuns in Connecticut who made dolls like mine . . . what were the chances? Wonder entered into my soul that God wanted to commune with me, little ridiculous me, to answer my objections in a detailed, totally personal way. It was like God saying, "Just step into the adventure, Stacey. I'll take care of you. Your needs and wants, even sculpting your dolls, are important to me."

Okay, God. You win. You've answered my objections. I'll go all in on discerning religious life. But for the record, I still don't want to.

I left the Abbey changed. I was at peace, knowing I was going to follow the adventure. Actively pursuing my questions led to resolution. While on paper my relationship with Mr. Catholic Musician should have been the answer to everything I wanted, dating him had proven otherwise. The breakup came soon after my visit to Regina Laudis, and I felt hugely relieved. While religious life didn't make sense intellectually to me, pursuing answers through action opened up a new possibility. I was gathering data to prove the right decision . . . to God? No, he already knew how this should go. I needed data to prove the right decision to myself.

Picture this: You go up to your room, light a candle, and get some lovely peaceful chant playing. Then you kneel down and ask God, "What do you want for my life?" Incense fills the room. You see a vision of a giant hand lowering from the heavens. The hand gives you a paper with step-by-step instructions for how your future will go. A voice booms, "I want you to do such-and-such. Oh, and you can marry so-and-so."

Don't you wish that's how God would speak? We all do. We all want to receive the answer without having to risk trying out things that turn out to be wrong. Getting to know ourselves through time and action is deep work. We want the answer *now*. That's just not how it works, and it's a very, very good thing.

GOD, THE PERFECT PARENT

God loves us like a good parent—the perfect parent, in fact! A good parent wouldn't choose a profession for his child and demand that he enter it. That would be ridiculous! God doesn't want us to be his servants. Rather, a good parent wants his child to choose something he's attracted to, that fits his natural abilities and talents. If the child chooses something that goes against the grain of his natural abilities, the parent is sad to watch him struggle, but his love isn't conditional. God often trusts us more than we want to trust ourselves. "For those who are led by the Spirit of God are children of God. For you did not receive a spirit of slavery to fall back into fear, but you received a spirit of adoption, through which we cry, 'Abba, Father!'" (Romans 8:14–15).

Although it can be frustrating when we need to take the "long way around" without a clear direction, God isn't just a passive bystander. When we take action to dispel a fear or follow a dream, God is encouraging us every step of the way. Just as a parent gets down on the floor and cheers a baby on as he learns to walk, God is cheering us on as we face our fears and get our questions answered. He is intimately interested in every twist and turn our path takes, and he doesn't tire of listening to us. We just need to take the action within our ability right now and trust he has good things in store for us. When we give God a "down payment" of patience and faith, we will eventually see that, no matter how insane life may feel, "All things work for the good of those who love the Lord and are called according to his purpose" (Romans 8:28).

YOUR ADVENTURE AWAITS: JOURNAL PROMPTS

When I interviewed Fr. Mike Schmitz on *Called and Caffeinated*, he put it perfectly and succinctly: "Action purifies desire." If you're a person of action like me, you'll find it easy (perhaps even too easy) to start doing something right away. Be wary, fellow go-getter friends, of running away too soon when something is hard!

But perhaps you're more naturally laid-back and tend toward inactivity. Type B people have many talents, but motivating yourselves to take action (especially uncomfortable action!) isn't usually one of them. Here's a strategy we all can do in fifteen minutes that will turn looming, unspecified wonderments into massive action.

- Take a deep breath, pray to the Holy Spirit, and write your need or question in the center of a sheet of paper. Draw a circle around it. For example, "Should I start my own business?"

- Now that you've written down your big question or need, break it down. Write down your questions around the middle question that you need to answer, and connect those smaller circles to the big middle one. Continuing the example above, you might write, "How much money will I make?" "How much time and money do I need to invest to get started?," and "Do I have enough experience to get started?"

🏔 Now you're working with specific questions. Think about how to begin answering them. Brainstorm the tasks you need to do to answer the secondary questions you just wrote. For example, in order to answer the question "How much time and money do I need to invest to get started?," you may want to write "research website costs," "talk to an entrepreneur who started a similar business," and "sign up for a course on starting a business." Do you see how specific and manageable your big goal becomes with these questions?

🏔 Set a goal immediately—don't wait until tomorrow, friend!—with a time frame for three things you can do, starting now. In the example above, you could resolve to carry out those three research and learning items within the next week.

🏔 As you move, keep praying and reflecting. Perhaps after the conversation with the entrepreneur, you bring that conversation to God and ask him to show you what he wants you to know. Did your heart burn with desire and excitement while the entrepreneur talked? Were you thinking, *I want to do that too*? Or did you hear his or her story and think, *Nope, that sounds like a challenge I don't want*?

🏔 Keep taking action until you've taken all the action steps in your brainstorm, and bring your discernment to prayer every day. Give the Lord time to unfold his plan. When you take action and continue trusting in him, he will!

4

VISIONS AND VOICES

HOW GOD SPEAKS DIRECTLY
AS A VOICE IN YOUR MIND

A clean heart create for me, God; renew within
me a steadfast spirit.
—Psalm 51:12

I am an overachiever, to put it mildly. You tell me I can't do something? I'm determined to do it better, longer, and harder than anyone else. In his divine humor, God decided to give me a double discernment challenge: He wanted me to discern religious life . . . then, I needed to discern whether God wanted me to discern religious life *on reality television.* Even for me, the ultimate go-getter, it was a lot.

As I slowly began to tell family and friends what I was thinking, I found a few reactions were helpful. Others were less so.

Many were dubious: "Why would you waste your life?" Others had the opposite reaction: "The Church needs more young people saying yes to vocations!" Either way, I felt stuck. *Great. I'm either a fool or the entirety of Christendom is relying on my yes . . . no pressure.* I suddenly felt as if I had a target on my back. I longed for the safety of having a boyfriend again. I had to learn to filter out the negative and overly positive voices and hear God's voice speaking to me.

Fortunately, God led me to a beautiful place to do just that: Domus Porta Fidei (translated "Home of the Gate of Faith"), a young-adult community located in a seminary-turned-retreat-center on Long Island. It was a new concept the rector wanted to try: bringing young adults to live in community while discerning God's will for their next steps. There were a dozen of us living there in one wing of the retreat house, which was stunningly beautiful, set on 250 breathtaking acres overlooking Long Island Sound. The facility could house up to two hundred people, and retreatants were constantly coming and going. We had daily Mass, four chapels to pray in, weekly spiritual direction available, and dinners together as a community. I only had to work twenty hours a week to make enough to live on, so I had abundant free time. It was a slice of heaven on earth.

During this time, I was learning two important lessons. First, when God calls you to face a difficult fear and you act on the call, he puts ground under your feet as you go. Even if it looks bleak at first, what you need appears the exact moment you step out. Second, God leads by beauty and attraction. My heart was enraptured by the beauty of this place—if my exodus from New York City led to wandering in this "desert," I was totally here for it!

A PRAYER OF SURRENDER

The retreat house was quiet most of the time, and with a light work schedule I passed my days serenely. Every morning, I took a five-mile walk and soaked up the ephemeral beauty of nature. I felt drawn to the gilded chapels and spent much time there. Away from the constant noise of my NYC life, I was learning to reflect and be silent. And as I learned silence, I came face-to-face with my greatest fear: surrendering my future to God.

I really felt I was at a crossroads. Following my theater dreams hadn't made me happy, and yet I was out of ideas of where to go next. I was grateful that God had delivered me from the evil voices in my head and that he had put me in an incredible place with good friends. He'd begun to show me that he could answer the desires of my heart, but I still didn't want to let go of control. I still bucked at the idea of becoming a nun. He had provided for me, answered prayers, and given me a glimpse of the adventure that awaited me. Now I had to decide whether I would reciprocate with trust before I knew the story's ending.

I did the thing that came most naturally to me: take action. I made an appointment to go to a weekend retreat with the Little Sisters of the Poor in Queens. I wanted a vocational discernment experience off-camera in case the reality show impeded my real-life discernment. I figured that if God told me I was done discerning religious life on that retreat, I'd be off the hook for the reality show.

Well, I loved the weekend at the convent. I hated that I loved it, but I couldn't deny it. The Sisters served the elderly in their nursing home, and I fell in love with their work. I soaked up hearing the residents' life stories, and they were thrilled to have someone listen. I cried and laughed with them, and I couldn't wait to pay another visit. I felt the same way I'd felt doing a week of service in the Bronx: at home with myself.

I still had many questions: Was I ready for the rule of obedience, where I could be stationed anywhere in the world and would almost entirely have to give up seeing my family? Would I like community life? Was I okay with getting up at five in the morning every day? Would I love this life more than having a husband and kids? Each of those questions needed to be answered. *Dang it*, I thought, *I'm in deep now. And I guess maybe I need to do the TV show.*

JOINING "THE SISTERHOOD"

Deep in doubt, I contacted the TV show producer to get more information. She told me that the nuns would have editing power over the episodes to take out anything they felt portrayed them in an undesirable light. That made me feel better about committing. Even though I didn't have editing power over myself, it showed me that they weren't out to make all Catholics look stupid, as I'd feared.

A friend tried to convince me to bow out of the show, out of caution that they'd make a fool of me. "They'll find someone to be in it, Stacey. Why does it have to be you?" I reflected a moment. "Well, why not me? If not me, then maybe my spot will be filled by someone who isn't actually discerning religious life." I remembered Mother Dolores's casual "Why not?" I couldn't explain it, but I felt somehow relaxed. I didn't like discerning, but the show felt like an adventure.

Right before filming began, my trust issues with the Lord came to a head. I went to Confession and confessed that I didn't

trust God with my future. The young priest said little; he nod-
ded and handed me a prayer on a holy card. He invited me to
pray it every day slowly. I looked at the card in my hand. There
was no author listed. It was titled "A Prayer of Surrender." (For
access to the full prayer please visit www.staceysumereau.com/
adventureawaitsbook.)

Pray it every day I did, and for weeks it was awful. The prayer
read like a litany:

> In Jesus's name, Father,
> I place myself entirely in your Heart.
> I surrender to you my whole self,
> My heart, my mind, my memory,
> My imagination, my will, my emotions . . .
> I surrender every person in my life to you.
> I surrender every situation in my life to you.
> I surrender every relationship I am in to you.[1]

I imagined God's hands outstretched toward me, and slowly
I'd put each part of myself in his hands. The prayer revealed
exactly what I was holding back from God. On any given day, I'd
be okay with handing him 70, maybe 80, percent. Some things
were even a relief to hand over. But there were always three, four,
or five things I wanted to cling to. *Why can't I keep control over
this? I've given you so much. Do I have to give you everything?*

Even as I said it, I knew the truth. If I truly believe God
knows all, and is all good, then yes, he deserves everything. If
I know myself in humility, then I'm the imperfect person in
this relationship. I can only benefit from giving it all to the One
who's perfect. So every day, I would burst into "ugly cries" as
I mouthed the last words of the prayer in the retreat center's
chapel:

O Most Holy Immaculate Virgin Mary.
I entrust this prayer to your heart.
Please help me to be as you are,
a perfect disciple,
an obedient servant,
a true child of God. Amen.

LIGHTS. CAMERA. ACTION.

Filming began. The first convent we visited was the Carmelite Sisters for the Aged and Infirm in upstate New York. Right from the first, I loved them. As I was spilling my anxieties to the vocation director, she laughed. "Don't worry, Stacey. We won't suck you in and keep you here. If you're not happy, trust me: we don't want you here, because we're the ones who'll have to live with you!" I chuckled and relaxed a little.

As the days passed, I began to understand how the Sisters' rhythm of life made sense. They had adequate time to pray every day. They were busy, but balanced. They had mission and deep peace. They were family to each other. I began to appreciate the beauty of religious life.

I still hadn't let go of my desire for marriage. I brought my favorite picture of Jesus with me in a frame. The strong, handsome portrayal of Jesus drew me in. I had to remind myself that, if I was going to give up an earthly husband, I was gaining a heavenly one! Not only was Jesus agreeable to look at, but his eyes were full of desire and compassion. His left hand extended toward the viewer, holding out his heart. It was the visual reminder I needed every day that Jesus wanted to help me work toward happiness, not block it. He didn't tire of listening to my struggles, and he wanted the best for me even more than I wanted it. The picture helped transfer my intellectual knowledge to my heart a little.

People often ask me what it was like having my discernment filmed. It was so many things at once: interesting, bizarre, difficult, fun at times, a work of evangelism, and a surrender of control. It was exhausting, but being on camera felt somehow natural. I was happy the producers were genuinely interested in filming our authentic experiences and didn't try to force anything. Of course, only the most dramatic 2 percent of what we filmed made it past the cutting-room floor and onto the final show. This is reality TV, people. Of *course* it's overdramatized! Certain moments were hyped up more in editing than when they actually happened, and critics of the show will always roll their eyes. I do myself, sometimes!

Being less reactive than others on the show, my story faded into the background somewhat in editing, which was totally fine with me. Later, one reviewer dubbed me "too well-adjusted for reality TV," and I took that as a compliment. My biggest regret? My hairstyle. The crunchy mousse curls make me cringe now. But hey, if that's the most I have to complain about, I'm fine with that.

The most interesting part of the show happened entirely off camera. The Sisters invited us to make a holy hour and attend Mass with them every morning before the camera crew arrived. I chuckle internally when I realize God's cleverness: If I hadn't signed a contract to stay at the convent until filming concluded, I may well have left early. Praying my prayer of surrender became unbearably arduous. I wanted to escape the thick, loaded silence of those holy hours. But I was stuck, and praise the Lord I was: it allowed him to give me the priceless gift he had in store.

AN EXCHANGE OF HEARTS

I'd never received visions or heard God's voice speaking to me like he did to the prophets. I'd always figured that was for holy people, so I didn't qualify. But one morning, that all changed. I followed my usual tradition: the prayer of surrender followed by my daily ugly cry. As I knelt with my eyes closed in the pew after Communion, Jesus appeared in front of me. He looked very much like my favorite painting. I was absolutely shocked. Suddenly, it was all real. Jesus was *here* with me. I wasn't surrendering to a void; I was surrendering to some*one*.

In the vision Jesus held out his heart to me, and my gaze fell to his heart as he held it out farther. He really wanted me to take it! Awestruck, I reached out and took his heart in my hand. Aware that there were no words for such a gift, I whispered breathlessly, "Thank you. What shall I do with it?" Jesus said gently, "Take out your heart, and put mine where yours used to be." I found I could open a small door in my chest I'd never noticed before by turning a latch.

I opened the door, reached in, and took out my heart. I put Jesus's heart where mine used to be, and I latched the little door closed. I could feel the warmth of his heart. I wept with the realization that the most perfect, loving, beautiful, all-powerful heart in the universe was mine. Jesus's heart *belonged* to me.

I looked down at my heart, still clasped in my hand. It was pathetic—gray, shriveled, and small. All my stingy self-preservation and small-mindedness were reflected in its appearance. *It's not at all how a human heart should look*, I thought. I looked up at Jesus. "What should I do with this?" With great desire in his eyes, Jesus said, "May I have it, please?" Inexplicably, he wanted my paltry little heart of stone. This wasn't a fair exchange at all!

I had received so much more than I could ever surrender, and he gave me his heart before I had ever promised him mine in return.

"You want *this*?" After receiving the enormity of the gift of his heart, I would have given him anything. But my pathetic heart, of all things? How could that be? I looked back to Jesus's eyes, and the depth of their desire and compassion reassured me that it was all he wanted. Weeping with gratitude and wishing I had more to give, I handed him my heart. He put my heart in the space where his used to be and closed the door in his chest. He was teary-eyed, too, but purely out of happiness.

As though looking through a clear glass door of a furnace, I could see my heart in his chest. As I looked, it burst into flame. Ezekiel 36:26 reads, "I will give you a new heart, and a new spirit I will put within you. I will remove the heart of stone from your flesh and give you a heart of flesh." That day, Jesus made that verse completely tangible and real for me. My relationship with the Lord would never be the same. Our relationship was no longer fraught with resistance, but flooded with peace and the belonging I had sought my whole life.

The vision couldn't have lasted more than ten minutes, but ten years later I still see it exactly as it happened. Its effects on my discernment were instantaneous. I now finally understood that the Lord only asked me to surrender my will in order that I might receive something much greater: himself. He wasn't trying to pry me from my dreams to give me a life I hated; rather, he wanted me to experience true happiness and purpose. He knew that he was the only One who could be my happiness. I finally understood how someone could want a life hidden away in a convent. Lo and behold, I suddenly wanted it too! Life in the convent wouldn't be imprisonment, but freedom and joy.

HOW DOES GOD'S VOICE ACTUALLY SOUND?

St. Teresa of Avila (1515–1582) was a Spanish nun who experienced many locutions from God, and she is considered one of the leading mystical authors in Church history. When visiting Rome, I was able to see the famous *Ecstasy of Saint Teresa* sculpted by Bernini. The otherworldly pleasure expressed on her face bespeaks the joy God imparted in revealing part of his kingdom to her.

When I discovered her guidelines on discerning locutions, I was excited to see that my experience aligned with what she wrote! In her spiritual colossus *The Interior Castle*, St. Teresa of Avila writes about discerning whether locutions (meaning visions and voices) come from God, the devil, or our own imagination.

First of all, we should be clear that receiving locutions such as visions and voices is by no means a reflection of holiness. St. Teresa wrote, "But of one thing I will warn you: do not think that, even if your locutions come from God, you will for that reason be any the better. After all, He talked a great deal with the Pharisees: any good you may gain will depend upon how you profit by what you hear."[2]

Many holy, faithful people I know have never received a vision or heard a voice from God; perhaps their faith is strong enough not to need them. After all, Jesus said, "Blessed are those who have not seen, but have believed" (John 20:29). If he gives me visions, it may well be because my faith is weak, not because I'm holy! My vision of exchanging hearts with Jesus was his answer to my crisis of trust, not a victory parade for perfect faith.

There are many ways for Jesus to speak to us—and this is *not* the way he does it most often. We should accept locutions not as an end to themselves, but rather as an impetus to spur us toward greater reciprocation of his grace through action.

Furthermore, St. Teresa of Avila emphasizes, it's extremely important to bring our potential locutions to a confessor or spiritual director and put them under his or her authority. If God seems to be telling you to do something, discussing it with a spiritual advisor can help you determine whether the message is something to be acted upon or ignored—that is, whether it comes from God, the devil, or your imaginative inventing.

Most visions or locutions I receive reveal some aspect of God's relationship with me or provision for me—for example, an image of Jesus on the Cross looking at me with love. He's not asking me to do anything, but rather simply wants me to know how much he loves me and for me to return his gaze. That kind of image aligns with what I already know to be true from scripture and the tradition of the Church, so I don't need to bring it to my spiritual director. I can accept it as a gift from God and allow it to lead me into a deeper trust in our relationship.

St. Teresa says some people hear a voice outside of themselves, spoken as if another person were in the room. What I received was an interior vision. No one else saw or heard the vision of me exchanging hearts with Christ. I'll attempt to describe how Jesus's voice "sounded" and how the vision "looked," although words will inevitably fall short.

Close your eyes and "see" a rose in your mind's eye. The experience of seeing my vision was a lot like that, although it differed in two important respects. First, the vision was clearer and felt more real than something I'd imagined. Jesus stood directly in front of me, not held in my mind the way the image of a rose is. Second, I didn't have the ability (or desire!) to jump away from what I was seeing at a moment's notice, as I can when I'm imagining things. Jesus was more "solid." Just as you can't whisk away a table to the next room using your thoughts, so I couldn't just make him "go away" by focusing my attention elsewhere.

The sound of Jesus's voice is equally tricky to describe. Imagine hearing one of your parents speak. Can you recall the timbre, accent, and pace? Can you "hear" it in your memory? Jesus's voice spoke through that memory space into my brain, so that I wasn't really "hearing" a voice outside myself, but rather recalling a memory of someone speaking. However, it was a voice I'd never heard before. It was like remembering something I never knew before.

OPENING YOURSELF TO A VISION FROM GOD

I never thought I was "holy enough" to receive a vision from God. After receiving the gift, however, I came to understand God wanted to meet me in a way I didn't expect, in order to break through my distrust and help me become holier.

As a speaker, I've shared my vision with thousands of people. My sharing opens up conversations about how we hear God speak. I've found that, like me, most Catholics don't expect to hear God speak as a voice or a vision. With that belief it's possible that we can begin to act as though we believe the "Watchmaker God" theory held by William Paley and other philosophers. The theory posits that God made and set creation in motion just as a watchmaker builds a watch, and God is letting it run its course without his further involvement. This is not what Christians believe. We believe God continues to be intimately involved with every aspect of creation, just as a good father continues to be available to his son for advice into adulthood.

Remember that when you pray, you're speaking to some*one*, not a void. God may actually reply! I encourage you to be open to his voice. Find an image of God that speaks to your heart, and look at it as you pray. My favorite picture is the Sacred Heart by Joseph Fanelli, but there are many beautiful portrayals of Jesus you can find in a quick Google search.

If you're not sure whether something you hear or see comes from God, you can enlist the help of both your spiritual director and St. Teresa of Avila's guidelines to discern it.

YOUR ADVENTURE AWAITS: JOURNAL PROMPTS

Throughout the history of the Church, saints have had heavenly visitors that appeared to them in the form of visions or locutions (audible messages) that are often referred to as "private revelations." Whether a message is for us alone or for the whole Church, it is important to discern carefully the source of that message.

St. Teresa of Avila offered her Sisters important guidelines to help them discern God's voice clearly. The full text of *Interior Castle* is worth your while to read, but I've compiled her main points from the Sixth Mansions chapter in modern English for a quick reference guide.

- Does the vision contradict anything the Church teaches, either in scripture or in her authoritative teaching (such as the *Catechism*)? If so, disregard the locution.

- Does the voice leave you feeling restless or peaceful? Do the words carry power and authority? For example, if you hear, "Be not afraid," do you immediately feel unafraid, as the words command?

- Do you forget the image and words quickly, or do they stay with you?

- Can you feel your imagination inventing the scene piece by piece, or is it something you wouldn't have imagined yourself?

- Look at the fruit of the vision (again, this might be best discussed with your pastor, confessor or spiritual director). Does it expand your understanding of spiritual matters?

Still not sure? Then it's time to take it to your pastor, spiritual director, or confessor. God puts these people in our lives to help us gain the clarity and spiritual insight we need, when we need it!

5

VALIDATION, NOT COMMANDS

DISCOVERING THE TRUE VERSION OF OURSELVES

Love, and then do what you will.
—St. Augustine

I once read a story about a man employed by a bank to find counterfeit bills. His son asked him how he could tell whether the bill was real or fake. The man answered that there are millions of versions of potentially counterfeit money. You can't study them all; rather, you can only find counterfeits by *studying the real thing.* When you know every intricate detail of real money, you can easily spot what's fake.

The vision of Christ giving me his heart was a landmark moment in my own spiritual journey. Afterward, many things I thought were true seemed counterfeit compared to what had passed between the Lord and me. I'd been shown ultimate love, and now I had to level up my mind and my habits to meet it. My deeply held assumptions, ingrained habits, and reactionary self-protection instincts needed to be sanctified. I began to realize how selfish I was and how long I had acted out of emotional poverty and fear. It was going to be a long process to integrate the wonderful love that had been initiated in me.

Filming *The Sisterhood: Becoming Nuns* continued. Just as God brought me Ana years before to help me process his love messages, so he now gave me another friend with a deep charismatic faith. Christie was no stranger to receiving locutions from the Lord. After the cameras left, we'd stay up long into the night discussing how the Lord was speaking to our hearts. Like me, she is a creative person. Because we shared similar love languages, it was exciting to witness similarities in the ways God was pursuing our hearts.

After two weeks with the Carmelites, we said a tearful goodbye and jetted off to Chicago. I believed the vision of Jesus was my call to religious life, and my heart was ready to say yes and find my order. I got very excited learning about the Daughters of St. Mary of Providence. They had no one particular work, such as teaching or serving the elderly; rather, their mission was to be a "mother, sister, and a friend to everyone." One Sister regaled us with tales of being assigned to convert gang members in Mexico! There were endless ways the Daughters could serve, and that sparked my sense of adventure and creativity.

Furthering my interest, I learned the Daughters were founded by St. Louis Guanella, an Italian saint. Every novice spent a year in Rome as part of her formation. *Rome*, I mused. *I've always wanted to visit Rome.* Spending a year soaking up the Lord's love surrounded by beautiful Roman architecture and art that I'd seen only in pictures sounded just absolutely thrilling to me. To top it off, Christie heard her call to join the Daughters during our visit. When she told me, we both wept with happiness. *Wouldn't it be amazing to join the same order together?* I thought.

Most people who discern religious life don't have cameras pointed in their faces with a TV producer querying, "What do you want to do with your life?" The downside of that kind of pressure is obvious, but there was an upside too: it forced me to deeply examine my desires. No escapism or schlepping through an unexamined life for me!

The show's focus revolved around what *I* wanted, putting me at the center of my universe. They didn't think to ask how I felt called to make a *gift* of my life. I was often presented with a counterfeit view of the world: to judge my vocation through the lens of what would *serve me according to whatever measure I chose.* I sensed I should have a deeper motivation, but my spiritual life needed maturation. To the producers' credit, they didn't force anything, but naturally they hoped we would choose one of the three orders we visited on the show. The third order we visited in Kentucky was a wonderful one, but I knew it wasn't where I belonged. As the days of filming drew to a close, I felt confident I should join the Daughters of St. Mary of Providence. I told my family on camera, and my heart was full of happiness.

Because the show would take several months to edit and air, the producers asked us not to spill the secret or enter the convent until the series finished. I flew back to Long Island to my quiet

haven at the retreat center. To my surprise, I arrived in the quiet
to find . . . disquiet. A new tension quickly arose.

The worm of discontent was back! I felt it as I thought about
entering as a postulant in Chicago. Something wasn't quite right,
and in all the silence I couldn't pretend it was. I felt betrayed.
*Lord, I'm willing to give you my life! I surrendered everything! You
gave me the most beautiful call I could have imagined. Why are
you playing a bait-and-switch with my heart? What am I supposed
to do? Just tell me!*

Jesus's reply was always both more *and* less satisfying than
I wanted. When I prayed, I listened desperately for an answer.
Every day the same words popped into my mind as I prayed: *Do
you know how much I love you?* I knew they were his words, not
mine, because if it were up to me, I would've ended the torture
and given myself an answer! Though I should have been nothing
but grateful, my desire for an answer *right this moment* made me
frustrated. I'd give a cursory, *Thank you, but what am I supposed
to do with that? Just tell me what to do!*

As the months unfolded, I realized that Jesus's words "Do
you know how much I love you" *were* my answer. His greatest
concern for me is not which vocation I choose, but for me to be
with him forever in heaven.

FREEDOM TO CHOOSE

As my desire for an immediate answer was slowly purified, I
realized God's desire was to first form my heart by love, and then
leave me free to choose my vocation. St. Augustine wrote, "Love,
and then do what you will." There's much to ponder in that pithy
statement. When we love God with a *true* love, we will choose

what God wants for us because our wills will be aligned with his. I wasn't quite there yet. I wanted God to dictate the plan to me because I didn't want the responsibility of potentially making a wrong choice. My desire for answers arose from an immature heart. I wanted God's answer more than God himself.

God, however, wants a love that's free. He refused to build me a prison like the one I'd occupied during the days of my eating disorder. He gently showed me his role in my life by the way he spoke to me: not as a taskmaster, but as a lover of my soul.

Fr. Jacques Philippe's words challenged me: "Our great drama is this: Man does not have confidence in God. Hence, he looks in every possible place to extricate himself by his own resources and renders himself terribly unhappy in the process rather than abandon himself into the tender arms of his Father in heaven." He goes on to assert, "How many young people, for example, hesitate to give their lives entirely to God because they do not have confidence that God is capable of making them completely happy."[1] As I read them, I underlined these words and in the margin wrote, "Me!"

It took a long time to get comfortable with the freedom God was offering me when I sought him rather than an answer to my discernment quest. Eventually I learned that holding the empty space in my heart without trying to fill it myself meant God could fill it. The emptiness hurt at first, but gradually it was filled. I began to understand the gentle whispers of God's voice as I went about my day.

One evening I gazed upon a gorgeous sunset. Clouds streaked the sky in a riot of pink, orange, and purple. I was amazed. What kind of God would create a show so ridiculously beautiful for no reason other than our enjoyment? *Thank you*, I prayed. Instantly his reply echoed in my mind: *I love you more than all of this.* A peace accompanied those words: *When he looks at me, I'm more beautiful to him than this sunset!*

God wanted his peace to permeate every area of my life, including and *especially* my vocational discernment. I was treating it as rules to decode, as if God's will is a puzzle. He didn't want me to leave my trust at the door as I wrestled inside with the big questions about my future. Instead, he wanted my trust to be the first and foremost attitude with which I approached my discernment. He was teaching me that discernment *is* relationship.

CALLED ... TO WHAT?

"The dignity of the human person is rooted in his creation in the image and likeness of God; it is fulfilled in his vocation to divine beatitude" (*CCC*, 1700).

Pause there.

The *Catechism* doesn't say your vocation is marriage or religious life or priesthood or to be a CEO or a lawyer or a plumber. *Our vocation is heaven, seeing God face-to-face.* When God speaks to us about our relationship with him rather than dictating a plan, he's gently preparing us for our eternal call.

In his exhortation *Christus Vivit*, Pope Francis wrote, "The word 'vocation' can be understood in a broad sense as a calling from God, including the call to life, the call to friendship with him, the call to holiness, and so forth. This is helpful, since it situates our whole life in relation to the God who loves us. It makes us realize that nothing is the result of pure chance but that everything in our lives can become a way of responding to the Lord, who has a wonderful plan for us" (no. 248).

It took me a long time to understand that while I'm called to a vocation as my path to heaven, more broadly and fundamentally I'm called to relationship and freedom.

My anxiety over my vocation increased as the months went on. I continued speaking to the vocation director for the Daughters about my desire for a husband and children. She told me that I needed to grieve those desires in order to enter religious life in a healthy way. That sounded awful. As I prayed further, I didn't want to grieve a husband and children I'd never have. Rather, I wanted them!

The questions the TV producers asked me focused on my preferences: Did I like the color and style of the habit? Did the Sisters' daily routine and work please me? Those were surface-level questions that didn't touch the deeper motivations for choosing a vocation.

In the pastoral constitution *Gaudium et Spes* Pope John Paul II wrote, "Man . . . cannot fully find himself except through a sincere gift of himself" (no. 24). In the quiet, the Lord was gently opening my eyes to a new reality: my deepest fulfillment, the deepest layer of my desire, is to give myself away. That's both my desire *and* God's desire for me. This is the great adventure: the risky but inexpressibly rewarding adventure of self-donation.

King Solomon was a man who, like me, knew he wasn't qualified to make the decisions before him (see 1 Kings 3). He had inherited the throne from his father David, who upon his death left behind him a complicated family that made a reality TV show appear tame! Furthermore, there were sins over inappropriate forms of worship going back generations that the Israelites needed to correct.

Solomon knew he needed to help his people and his family level up, but he didn't know how. God appeared to Solomon in a dream and offered to give him whatever he wanted. We can all learn a lot from his reply: "Now, Lord, my God, you have made me, your servant, king to succeed David my father; but I am a mere youth, not knowing at all how to act—I, your servant, among the people you have chosen, a people so vast that it cannot be numbered or counted. Give your servant, therefore, a listening heart to judge your people and to distinguish between good and evil. For who is able to give judgment for this vast people of yours?" (1 Kings 3:7–9).

God was pleased with his request. "Because you asked for this—you did not ask for a long life for yourself, nor for riches, nor for the life of your enemies—but you asked for discernment to know what is right—I now do as you request. I give you a heart so wise and discerning that there has never been anyone like you until now, nor after you will there be anyone to equal you" (1 Kings 3:11–12).

Why was God pleased with Solomon's request? He was pleased because Solomon was wise to ask for wisdom and a right attitude of heart first. He knew answers would flow from that wisdom, and he desired it more than any material comfort or glory for himself. I was slowly learning to desire a listening, discerning heart first and foremost. When I finally stopped fixating on an answer and set my priority higher, the answer came.

Here's the kicker to the Solomon story: not only did he get the discerning, listening heart he asked for, but he got everything he didn't ask for too! A peaceful, prosperous reign, wealth and glory for himself, and a long, happy life. Solomon amazed people with his wisdom, so that other rulers sought out his wisdom and friendship.

HANDLING ANXIETY OVER CHANGING DIRECTION

It slowly dawned on me that I was idolizing my vocation first and putting God second. As I learned to focus on the Lord and fear people's judgment less, my counterfeit motivations began to fall away.

Would viewers of the show call me nasty names online if I changed my path? Possibly . . . but this was no reason to choose religious life. Similarly, I had to let go of my people-pleasing desire to be someone "who finally said yes and began a new wave of religious vocations to save the Church!"

Even motivations that weren't bad, in and of themselves—such as my desire to spend a year in Rome or to join because Christie was joining—were not good-enough reasons for joining religious life. Neither was my desire to "stick with the plan" simply because it'd be less emotionally exhausting than pivoting away from an established path and back into the unknown.

It took time, but the truth came out again and again in conversations with trusted friends, my parents, and my spiritual director: *What does it really matter what anyone thinks of you? Only you are living your life. God is okay with you being a work in progress, so everyone who cares about you will be too.*

Love God first, then do what you will. More weeks in prayer taught me I wanted to be married and have children. I finally realized that, scary as it was for me to step out into the unknown again, he was asking me to choose how I wanted to make a gift of my life.

So, one day in the chapel, I took a shaky breath in and a long, slow exhale. *Okay, God. I've given you almost a year discerning my vocation. I've visited five convents and prayed a holy hour and Mass every day to listen for your voice. I don't know for sure what you want, but I trust you'll take care of me. I'll give you one more month of discerning religious life, and after that if I still want to be married as much as I do now, then I'll be open to dating again. Please guide my heart as you want it to go.*

A month went by, and I continued to go to Mass and make a daily holy hour. By the end of the month, my desire for marriage and children had grown. I felt my desire had been confirmed.

It was around that time that I was heartened to read about two married saints—Louis and Zélie Martin (the parents of my Confirmation saint, Thérèse of Lisieux!), who discerned wrong initially but ended up finding the vocation God intended for them. Louis wanted to be a priest but found it too hard to learn Latin. Zélie wanted to be a nun but was told to leave the convent, without explanation, by the Mother Superior. After their rejections, they met while crossing a bridge, and Zélie heard God say to her that she would marry Louis. If they loved God fully but still discerned the wrong vocations initially, I have some leeway to mess up too!

The show finally aired, and I got my "five minutes of fame," interviewing on *Fox and Friends*, *The Today Show*, and *Access Hollywood*. And guess what? None of my worst fears about being judged as flaky came true. Sure, there were haters on Twitter (what else can you expect from the internet?). But in general, viewers both religious and secular concurred that finding your path is a journey with no map, in which there are bound to be dead ends and wrong turns.

YOUR TRUE SELF

Since the 1970s, a fascinating body of research has emerged on what scientists term "the true self." Research has shown that people overwhelmingly believe that a "true," central version of everyone exists. That central self is morally good, cross-culturally stable, and perspective independent (meaning the self is objective and not skewed in its outlook). Immoral actions betray, but do not destroy, this true self. A murderer, for example, betrays himself when he engages in the heinous act of taking innocent life; however, people believe that deep down his true self is still good. If he repents, does his time in jail, and amends his ways, he is moving closer toward uncovering his true self.[2]

While scientists cannot prove that this "true self" actually exists, I find it fascinating that, even in our cynical internet age, people from a wide variety of backgrounds and religious beliefs still *think* the true self exists. The "true self" concept meshes perfectly with the tenets of the Catholic faith. We read in Genesis 1:31 that "God looked at all that he made, and found it very good." Discerning God's will moves us closer and closer to the more authentic, true self at our core.

From ten years in discernment ministry, I know that the most difficult part of discerning is that we have to let go of something good in order to say yes to a greater good. Moral teaching and conscience inform us when something is intrinsically evil or immoral, such as cheating on a spouse or a test. Therefore we only discern between options that will be good, better, or best. Discernment quickly reveals any gaps in experience, prudence, and self-knowledge.

When I was discerning my call to religious life (or marriage), God's communications with me never directed me absolutely, explicitly toward one course; rather, our two-way exchange of prayer helped me to discern my calling by appealing to my higher self. You might say that he speaks to me as my true self: the most noble, virtuous, purpose-driven, fully alive version of me.

YOUR ADVENTURE AWAITS: JOURNAL PROMPTS

Picture your inner "true self" described in this chapter. (It may help to close your eyes and imagine yourself going about your day.) What qualities does that most virtuous version of you possess? Here are some journal prompts to get you started.

- ▲▲ How would your true self handle your stresses, relationship issues, and difficulties? Who would you forgive? Who would you help, and how?

- ▲▲ Have you ever experienced a sense of gain after giving something away (possessions, time, effort, or skill)? What specific ways can you think of to give of yourself in your current situation?

- ▲▲ Do you worry about others' judgment or about losing time or resources if you make a change? Are those potential losses a good enough reason not to make the change? If in doubt, imagine the most compassionate friend you have. Write yourself a letter of advice from that friend's perspective about your current situation. Then take the advice that friend "gave" you!

- ▲▲ What counterfeit motivations did this chapter help you identify in your own life and discernment?

6

GOD WILL MEET YOU IN THE BIG DREAM

HOW GOD AFFIRMS US WITH NODS OF GRACE

You pay God a compliment by asking big
things of him.
—St. Teresa of Avila

When my television show aired worldwide, every week I
live-tweeted the show, interacting with my fellow discerners,
real-life sisters, and fans. It was surreal, watching myself on the
screen: I sweated through each episode, since I dislike watching myself on camera. Overall, though, I was pleased with the

results. Hundreds of messages poured into my social media inboxes from young people from around the world with whom my story resonated: *How did you know what God was calling you to? How did you hear him speak?* I realized that I wasn't the only one lacking in discernment formation.

Unfortunately, my testimony about the prayer of surrender and receiving Jesus's heart hadn't made it past the cutting-room floor. Maybe if they'd caught me levitating or had witnessed the vision, they would have included it. But no one had seen a thing, and I soon discovered the producers hadn't found my testimony "sensational enough."

And yet, it had changed the course of my life. Those chapel offerings had taught me that surrender is the secret key to our relationship with God, and that was the real story I wanted to tell.

Once the show had finished airing, I had a slew of new followers on social media, and I had a new mission. There were only two problems: I didn't know how to start sharing my story, and I didn't feel qualified to speak as an expert. *God forbid anyone think I actually knew what I was doing!*

I've heard the quip, "God doesn't call the equipped; he equips the called." I wish I could give the person who said that a medal! The fire was lit in my heart. I had many questions about my future, but I wasn't afraid of discernment anymore. I wanted to take the people who shared my fears and questions along with me and show them they had nothing to fear by surrendering. Knowing how God's speaking to me had changed my life, I wished I could help others hear his voice, too, and see the change in their lives.

Two months after the airing of *The Sisterhood* concluded, I hopped on a plane to my first Catholic conference in Nashville.

I had no idea what I was in for. I'd never been to a Catholic conference. A friend at the young-adult community where I lived had set up my ticket to help advertise the community and to recruit new members. When I arrived, many fans of the show recognized me. I cracked up seeing a group of seminarians freak out as they passed me in a hallway. "Your show was playing on a loop in our common room for weeks!"

During the four conference days, I attended every talk I could. I was amazed by what I heard. *There's a Catholic speaking world out there? An entire alternate universe of Catholic motivational speakers? This is what I want to do!* My heart burned within me. Did I feel wise enough to present to other people? Absolutely not! Did I still think I was called to do it and want to? Yes.

I had to smile at God's wink in my direction: *Remember how worried you were that the years you dedicated to theater were a waste? I can use everything.* With my theater training, I knew how to spin a comedic yarn, hit a punch line with pizzaz, and share my heart with vulnerability. Ideas popped into my head of adding singing into my presentations and perhaps some of the random special skills I had picked up in my theater days, such as eating fire. The challenge, I knew, would be depth of content. I had no doctorate in theology, and I was still synthesizing all the lessons I'd learned in my year of vocational discernment. I needed to study, reflect, and soak in all the wisdom I could find. I couldn't wait to get started.

I had a free day to tour Nashville after the conference. I tried to motivate myself to see the sights, but my heart couldn't hold it in any more. I had to start getting my ideas on paper. I found the nearest lunch spot, ordered a barbeque sandwich, and spilled it all out on paper. I wrote for two hours nonstop. When the time came to depart for the airport, I stood up with a sigh. *I think I've found the next layer of the onion.*

To use my theater skills for the glory of God: that was a thing worth doing! I began to deepen my personal study and seek resources on how to craft talks. I didn't care that I was investing time for no monetary return; the art and play of learning to be a speaker fascinated me.

A few weeks after I got back from Nashville, a message came in: "Hey, Stacey, I'm an organizer for the National Catholic Youth Conference. I saw on social you were just at a conference, and I saw you on *The Sisterhood*. Would you consider coming to speak at NCYC in November?" I caught my breath. An opportunity to present my story at a big conference! *Wow! Thank you, Lord.*

Each time God speaks or intervenes in our lives is a miracle, but that doesn't mean it's rare. My whole life before receiving the vision of Christ's heart, I had treated my faith like superstition. If God wasn't sending me a sign that defied the laws of nature, such as writing in the sky or talking through a burning bush, then he wasn't acting or speaking. My assumptions were based on a too-limited image of God: a God who wanted his subjects to get in line, or else hellfire and brimstone for you! It was an image I'd trapped in the vestiges of a dusty Bible on my shelf that I never read.

Consequently, I never gave God an inch to work in my life. I didn't allow myself to need him. After being brought to my knees by my inability to fulfill myself, I had nowhere to go but surrender. Surrender led to trust. Trust led to a new image of God: a God who speaks to me in many creative ways, who wants to provide for me, and who loves me more than I love myself. I was learning to take 1 Peter 5:7 to heart: "Cast all your worries upon him, because he cares for you."

The suspicion that maybe God isn't *that* good still hung around . . . in fact, the temptation to think this way still hits me from time to time. The devil tempted Eve in the Garden of Eden to believe that God was withholding godlike status from her, keeping her firmly in second place behind him. Not much has changed since Eden! It's easy to be grateful when prayers are answered in a quick and amazing way, such as my being invited to speak at a national conference when I desired a speaking ministry. It's easy to praise the Lord and be in awe of his majesty and the way he meets us in the deep longings of our hearts. It's much harder to trust when we experience the longing and don't see an answer yet.

In times of waiting on the Lord, I need to call myself back to remembrance of the many small miracles and communications he has given me. It's astounding to me how quickly and often I can forget the wonders he's worked in my life and return to my default suspicion!

WHEN GOD CLEARS THE WEEDS

My journey toward hearing the Lord speak to me didn't originate with a grand vision; it started with healing from my wounds—a lifelong work in progress, honestly—and finding out what I didn't want. He had to clear the weeds in order to plant the seeds.

Still imperfect though I was, seeds of interior freedom had taken root enough to begin to give myself away. My speaking was still a slow process of purification. At first, I translated much of my theater ambition onto a speaking career. It was too much about Stacey being popular, Stacey making people laugh and cry,

Stacey booking engagements at impressive venues. I didn't even realize it at first! Thank God for his patience.

As I was preparing for my first big speaking engagement, someone challenged me to a dreaming exercise. "What would you do if you had no limitations on your time, energy, or resources?" she asked. I gave a quick answer, something that felt comfortable: fitting in a workout daily, taking time to prepare healthy meals, getting enough rest, and so on. My friend wasn't satisfied. "What about all your bigger goals?" she pressed. "I know you have them. Where do they fit in? Remember, pretend you have no limits whatsoever!"

I tried to think bigger. It was a struggle. I was shocked at how accustomed I was to limiting myself, even in my imagination, to what I could reasonably accomplish. Everyone thought of me as a dreamer for going after my Broadway career in New York, but that was a preexisting career. Instead I was being invited to imagine a kind of life that exceeded my own ambitions—something I had never thought possible.

Young-adult ministry in the Catholic Church is lacking, with few national organizations to serve the specific needs of the young-adult community. At the parish and diocesan levels, funds are usually allocated toward sacramental preparation (especially Confirmation) and toward high-school students. However, college-campus ministry and young-adult ministry usually serve a relatively small population in most parishes. Often, they can't afford to bring speakers out. I was going to have to find a new way to reach the young adults I felt called to serve. This was my big dream. Isaiah 43:19 says, "See, I am doing something new! Now it springs forth, do you not perceive it? In the wilderness I make a way, in the wasteland, rivers."

THE "GOD NOD"

The solution to my dilemma wouldn't emerge for a while as I continued to think outside the box, imagining a future with unlimited goals. Some of the things I wanted weren't particularly holy—a home dance studio, for example—but I wrote them down anyway. I was learning that it's important not to censor our dreams. After all, my Broadway dreams weren't holy, but they pointed the way to something that was holy: a passion for community and furthering God's kingdom. If I edited my dreams before they ever had a chance even to be written down, how could God work with those desires? No, honesty was the way to go.

I was learning a new way that God speaks. I'll call it the "God nod." It's an interior or exterior confirmation that you're on the right track. An exterior God nod to my desire to be a speaker was the invitation to speak at the national conference. That was an easy one! But there were many more subtle ones along the way. I felt an interior God nod confirming my desire to speak when I watched other speakers and gained from their wisdom. I felt an affirmation that my work was needed when I received questions from young adults seeking guidance for their wonderments about their future vocations. And I felt the same deep, affirming peace after I finished a talk, knowing I brought my whole heart to it.

I was keenly aware of my past and present sins and my lack of qualifications to speak. At times I felt like an imposter. I was used to having lines given to me; writing a forty-five-minute talk of completely my own content was extremely daunting.

My first iterations of a talk on discernment were less than inspiring. I'd get nervous and go down irrelevant rabbit holes that left people confused. Once when I gave a talk on a dry winter day, a coughing fit forced me to leave the stage and come back. My eyes were watering when I resumed, and there was a catch in my throat; I sounded like Yoda for the rest of the talk. I felt humiliated. Nevertheless, I knew that discernment formation was desperately needed, just as I had needed it. I persisted and kept looking for opportunities to speak. Paid or free—if I could do it, I did it.

I was getting a glimpse, finally, of what motivated the great saints to give everything for God. Mother Teresa's feet were malformed because she always gave her shoes away to the poor she loved. St. Paul underwent at least five scourgings and imprisonments, multiple shipwrecks, and finally martyrdom for the Lord he loved. The cross and the humiliations and the work, day in and day out, were all for love. It was all to fill a need in the kingdom of God. I was (and am!) far from being St. Paul or Mother Teresa, but I can attest to the addictive peace you experience by living your purpose.

Years later, I'd carved out a ministry—which had connected me with some of the smartest, holiest, and most interesting humans imaginable—through speaking and my podcast *Called and Caffeinated*. At times I've spoken on grand national stages and hosted online conferences reaching thousands of people. Other times I've written blog posts that reached only a few. God sends me these opportunities, and it has all evolved slowly and involved lots of failure, which has had a purifying effect on my pride and ambition. I wouldn't trade it for the world. It's part of my purpose and my contribution.

So where are you feeling your "God nod"? What opportunities are you being given to help other people along the path to holiness? Your purpose isn't just to be generally "holy" in a way that is uninteresting and bland to you. It is intimately connected to what you love to do, your talents, and the activities you enjoy for hours on end. What do you love to think about when you're not thinking of anything else? What do you lose track of time doing? What work would you do for zero money, simply because you love it for its own sake? Those things are all connected to God's will for you. Your purpose should fascinate you, delight you, terrify you with its hugeness, and capture your imagination.

I came across this beautiful piece by Fr. Joseph Whelan, SJ, attributed to Pedro Arrupe, which captures the spirit perfectly:

> Nothing is more practical than
> finding God, than
> falling in Love
> in a quite absolute, final way.
> What you are in love with,
> what seizes your imagination, will affect
>   everything.
> It will decide
> what will get you out of bed in the morning,
> what you do with your evenings,
> how you spend your weekends,
> what you read, whom you know,
> what breaks your heart,
> and what amazes you with joy and gratitude.
> Fall in Love, stay in love,
> and it will decide everything.[1]

Your purpose is always something big and grand in God's kingdom, but not necessarily big and grand in this world. A mother changing her baby's diapers and serving her family three meals a day is doing worthy work by heaven's standards. A father directing his ambition toward providing for his family's needs and serving his community is rich in the kingdom. A single person who gives time to the needy in his or her community is making worthy effort in God's eyes. The more you pursue God, the more he will form your heart to look like his, so that your ambition is both increased and pointed in the right direction. Start with uncensored dreaming, and bring it to God.

For some, dreaming big will come naturally. For others it'll feel like a real stretch or even wrong. I know some wonderful, practical-minded people who have resisted the idea of dreaming. "What's the point?" they say.

Dreaming aligns us with God's vision. God dreams bigger than our reality! He wasn't thinking, "What's the point?" when he made sunsets spectacular or the stripes on an iris so intricate. He also doesn't look at you as the sum of your failures or your successes. He sees you in the light of eternity and in light of your full potentiality. Don't worry; if your dreams are supposed to be lived out, God will bring them about. And then you'll see the "point" of dreaming was to align your vision with his, to motivate you to accomplish more than you would have by staying stuck in a to-do list.

FR. MIKE ON ORDERING YOUR LIFE

Sometimes people can resist dreaming because they worry it'll take them away from their legitimate duties and obligations. That would be possible if you didn't surrender your dreams to God. When I interviewed Fr. Mike Schmitz on the *Called and Caffeinated* podcast, he discussed the three levels of our callings:

- first, our call to holiness and heaven;
- second, the call to our vocation; and
- third, the call to everything else.

We are obliged to keep our callings ordered. For example, parents' side hustles or hobbies shouldn't take priority over the call to serve their children and spouse. Similarly, a person's love for his spouse should be secondary to his love for God. While I believe we shouldn't judge our dreams, even the superficial ones, we also shouldn't *act* on those dreams until we have surrendered and ordered them to our life's circumstances.

Dreaming is wild territory, there's no question. Lest you worry that your dreams will lead you to abandon your children and fly off to Timbuktu, let me explain further. My outlook is that dreams will ultimately take you closer to and intertwine with your proper state in life. If you're a parent who loves her family, your work outside the home (should you choose to engage in it) will enrich and inform your marriage and family life, and vice versa. Each person's calling is unique.

A close friend of mine has a dream of homeschooling her ten children. Her passions are classical education and household economy, and she executes both well. She has informally but powerfully helped many people in our community to gain a more peaceful, disciplined household. I'm in awe of how her gifts are used to form an intentional, faithful family culture, and her legacy will be all the love and generosity with which she served her children and community. She is living her dream, and everyone who knows her witnesses her purpose, passion, and peace.

THE DREAM IS THE DOING, NOT THE RESULT

My encouragement to "dream big" is not an uncommon one. Unfortunately, I see some Christian influencers miss important nuances in their writings on dreaming and goal setting. Their focus is too narrow. When they tell their followers to expect to see all the results of their efforts, it creates an unrealistic expectation of achieving glory in this life. The result will be discouragement if the dreams don't "manifest" as well as an overemphasis on external validation as the measure of the dream's worth. God's plan may be to wait for glory in heaven.

Living a surrendered life means God delivers results in his time and in his way. I absolutely love hearing from my listeners that my ministry has helped them find their path! However, I always have to realize that the dream is so big that no statistics or results, either positive or negative, will ever be the true measure of the worth of my ministry dream—or yours. God sees every effort we make for his kingdom, and he does not judge our "success" by tangible ministry results. All we're called to do is what's in our control. Effort is in our control; results are God's department.

Let's say you start a spiritual podcast that only gets twenty downloads an episode (just as *Called and Caffeinated* did when I started producing it). You love making the podcast, and you feel totally alive and energized by it, but the external results—the numbers—aren't very impressive. However, you persist, and your podcast reaches someone who's fallen away from faith. After tuning in, they're inspired to give the Catholic Church another try. When you reach your final judgment, God will say, "Well done, good and faithful servant."

My pastor likes to say, "Pray as if everything depended on God, and then work as if everything depended upon you." It's important to know that the *process* of working for the dream, not the result, should be what lights your heart on fire. The dream should be so big you could never see the end of it in your lifetime, but you can have the most fulfilling life by getting after it as hard as you can in the time you're given.

I think of the story of St. Carlo Acutis, an Italian teenager born in 1991 who called the Eucharist "my highway to heaven." Carlo's dream was to see all the Eucharistic miracle sites of the world and document them on a website. Back then the internet was still fairly new, and it took real skill to program a website. As a teenager who didn't enjoy enough autonomy yet to plan his own travel, Carlo made a few Eucharistic pilgrimages but had many more to go. He worked for two and a half years to set up the website. I can imagine the joy (and possibly frustration!) he felt chipping away at his work in the evenings after he finished his homework.

Just days before launching his website, fifteen-year-old Carlo became ill. On October 2, 2006, he was diagnosed with leukemia, and just ten days later he was dead. He never got to see the results of his hard work or the Eucharistic miracle sites. From an earthly perspective, his story is a tragic one. But from a heavenly perspective, Carlo's story is glorious. His home is heaven, which you could say is the ultimate Eucharistic miracle! In his memory, two bishops collaborated to produce a touring Eucharistic miracle presentation using the images and text from Carlo's website. To date the presentation has toured to more than ten thousand places in the world (including my home parish in Virginia). Even though he never saw the results, Carlo's work was not wasted; in fact, God multiplied it. Carlo's story reminds me of Proverbs 16:9: "The human heart plans the way, but the Lord directs the steps."

YOUR ADVENTURE AWAITS: JOURNAL PROMPTS

Now it's your turn. Below are some powerful journaling prompts to help you get started dreaming about your future. Remember, dreaming isn't a one-time exercise; it's a habit. I recommend taking time regularly—say, once a week—to return to your big-picture dreams.

Remember, don't judge them. Keep a journal only you will read so you're not tempted to censor yourself, and always pray the prayer of surrender from chapter 4 after a dreaming session. You'll be amazed in a few years to look back and see what God has done with your life!

- What do you want right now? Start with the first things that occur to you, then keep going deeper. Write everything down, and don't judge it.

- What would you do if you could do anything: no limitations of time, money, or energy?

- Finish the sentence: "Wouldn't it be amazing if . . .?" Finish the sentence for each area of your life: work, relationships, friendships, family, spiritual life, property, dreams, money, and time.

- What do you wish you could change in the world?

- What do you want your legacy to be?

- Who inspires you most? What is it about them you want to emulate?

7

LOVE NOTES
IN THE WAITING

AN INTRODUCTION TO
IMAGINATIVE PRAYER

Tell aching mankind . . . to snuggle up to my
merciful heart.
—Jesus to St. Faustina Kowalska

Do me a favor, would you? Try not to think of a purple elephant.
Just don't even think about it. Pause for a moment, close your
eyes, and don't imagine a purple elephant.

I'm guessing all you could think about was a purple elephant,
right?

Isn't it funny how our minds fixate on the thing we're told not to do, or have, or think? That's absolutely true for so many of us. When we want something, it's all we can think about. If there is no way to obtain it, frustration results. And too often, God gets the blame.

Life had been moving fast for a long time, and it finally slowed down. The reality show was done, and I had discerned that I was not called to religious life. I believed I was called to marriage, yet I had no prospects in that direction. The Carmelite Sisters I had discerned with on the TV show offered me a remote job with the educational department of their order, and I spent my days working alone in the quiet retreat house. I had booked my first big speaking engagement, which was still months away. Days at the retreat center felt arid. I felt stuck. No eligible young men serenaded me under my balcony . . . in fact, I even lacked a balcony. The desire for my husband grew and grew.

WEDDING BELL BLUES

Once again, I found myself falling prey to the temptation to put all my hopes for happiness in a future condition. I thought my "real life" could start once I had my husband. Now I look back and feel embarrassed at how envious I was of my friends who were in stable relationships. Lack of companionship shouldn't have been the thief of my joy, but it was. I hated hearing the phrase "all in God's timing." *Haven't I worked hard long enough to discern my vocation and put God first? Shouldn't he "reward" me with a relationship?* I fumed.

Sadly, I was to discover that although New York City has one of the largest concentrations of single young-adult populations in the world, it's also one of the hardest places to meet a spouse. I had hundreds of friends, but few interested in marriage. Because nearly everyone had moved to the city for a career, pursuing said career was the priority. I grew tired of single going-out culture and of waiting.

Thinking about timelines increased my anxiety. I was twenty-six; I thought by that time I'd have my life a bit more figured out! *Once I meet a guy it'll take three years to get to know each other . . . then at least a year of engagement before marriage . . . and who knows how long it'll take to get pregnant? I won't start having babies until I'm at least thirty-five, and by that time my dream of a big family will have passed me by.*

Once more, I secretly suspected that God wasn't truly good—that he was withholding the things that would make me truly happy and fulfill my true potential (a lie that goes all the way back to Eden). It's easier to be grateful when prayers are answered spectacularly and swiftly, such as my desire for a speaking ministry being validated with an invitation to a national youth conference. It's much harder to trust when we experience a longing that is not immediately gratified—when God says, "Wait."

REMEMBER TO BE THANKFUL

In times of waiting on the Lord, it helps to look back upon our lives and recall the many miracles, large and small, that God has given. The more we do that, the more we can have peace in the waiting.

Our mind is a battlefield. As St. Joan of Arc said, "All battles are first won or lost in the mind." First comes awareness of the suspicion that has crept into our minds and has accused God unjustly. Then we speak the truth that drives out error and mistrust. Finally, we must sincerely surrender our hearts to him, asking his help in resisting evil thoughts.

In the months of waiting for God to bring my future spouse into my life, I read a meditation by Pierre Teilhard de Chardin, SJ, titled "Patient Trust":

> Above all, trust in the slow work of God.
> We are quite naturally impatient in everything
>   to reach the end without delay.
> We should like to skip the intermediate stages.
> We are impatient of being on the way to some-
>   thing unknown, something new.
> And yet it is the law of all progress
> that it is made by passing through some stages
>   of instability—
> and that it may take a very long time.
> And so I think it is with you;
> your ideas mature gradually—let them grow,
> let them shape themselves, without undue
>   haste.
> Don't try to force them on,
> as though you could be today what time
> (that is to say, grace and circumstances acting
>   on your own good will)
> will make of you tomorrow.
> Only God could say what this new spirit
> gradually forming within you will be.
> Give Our Lord the benefit of believing
> that his hand is leading you,

and accept the anxiety of feeling yourself
in suspense and incomplete.[1]

Although I couldn't see what God was doing at the time, he was doing vitally important work in my time of waiting. Remember how I shared in chapter 3 that action allows us to gather data to prove the right decision to ourselves? Waiting does too. Action comes naturally to me, so it's my preferred method of data gathering, but in this instance, only waiting could prepare me for marriage.

I needed to be emptied. My whole adult life had been action-packed. I'd jumped at career opportunities, prioritizing those over relationships. I'd crammed my evenings with social events—sometimes party-hopping to two or three per night. I regularly overscheduled myself, and I saw no problem with it. I had so many ways to fill my heart with company and entertainment that I wasn't ready to settle into the dedication and work of marriage and family life.

The months of loneliness clarified and purified my desires. I went out with friends in groups but longed for a cozy night in with my husband. I was tired of many surface-level friendships and craved just a few intimate ones. I became ready to forsake constant entertainment. Don't get me wrong: I'll always be an extrovert, but party Stacey needed big-time interior change. Walking through months of loneliness was a gift to my future marriage.

Did I do it with the best attitude? Nope, absolutely not. I missed many opportunities to find the fulfillment God was offering me in his love. Old habits die hard, and my distrust of the Lord hadn't leveled up fully. Thankfully, I didn't miss all the opportunities. I remembered how happy the nuns on the show were, and how they looked for evidence of God's love everywhere. They had great confidence that, as their spouse, he wanted to send them "love notes" daily. One Sister said that on her really rough days, whoever was cooking for the community always happened to serve spaghetti and meatballs. It was her favorite meal, and she said it always lit her up to receive her favorite meal as a gift from her spouse. The same Sister also felt a great desire to be close to the Eucharist. In every new convent where she was assigned, she somehow always managed, through no effort of her own, to land in the room closest to the convent chapel. She called it God's way of "spoiling" his beloved.

Remembering the Sisters' stories, I began to (imperfectly) lean on the Lord. Leaning on him meant praying the prayer of surrender, attending Mass, and making a holy hour as often as possible—in my case, daily was usually possible because of my unique living situation at the retreat center. Just as I had learned to bring my whole self, messiness and awkwardness included, into my vocational discernment, now I needed to continue to bring my whole self to God in prayer and trust. God knew what was going on in my heart anyway, so no point in hiding!

The hardest part of being real with God is acknowledging how needy I am. I want to be in control. I cringe when I admit my own vulnerability and lack of power to conjure up what I want. I hated wanting marriage so much. It would be easier not to feel the loneliness, I thought. Sometimes I still wished I could go back to my old ways: just present my Sunday self to God and keep the messiness on lockdown, sequestered away both from myself and from him.

Yet my true self knew my relationship with the Lord had deepened and there was no going back. Thank God there was no going back! After my vision of receiving Christ's heart, I knew putting up walls couldn't lead to happiness. Presenting messy Stacey to God gave him the opportunity to heal the mess and show me I'm lovable and beautiful to him.

THE COLLOQUY

Making a holy hour most of my life consisted of stiffly reciting one rote prayer after another, a reflection of my overly narrow image of God. As my understanding of God grew in my vocational discernment, my prayer gradually expanded into a more authentic conversation. I discovered St. Ignatius of Loyola's *Spiritual Exercises*, a treasure trove of spiritual wisdom that breathed structure into the imaginative prayer I was experiencing. The *Exercises* contain several dozen meditations on the life of Christ, followed by what St. Ignatius calls a "colloquy." That's not an exotic French appetizer, but rather a fancy word for conversation. The colloquy is a simple way to enjoy daily, heart-to-heart quality time with God.

First, it takes discipline to put away my phone and ignore all the "necessary" interruptions that inevitably come to mind during prayer. (Somehow the only time I can remember my full to-do list is when I'm trying to pray!) But I find it's truly vital to shut down distractions and give God my full attention. Listening is the only way to hear! If it's hard to switch out of "go" mode, taking slow, deep, intentional breaths helps calm me. Using either the scripture readings for Mass for the day, my personal scripture reading, or one of St. Ignatius's meditations, I begin by imagining myself in the scene with Jesus.

I envision the scene in my mind's eye: the surrounding landscape, the feel of the air, the smells, and all the details of the scene. This immersive, imaginative experience will help make the story real. After watching the scene play out, I enter into the colloquy.

St. Ignatius's description of the colloquy is to imagine standing in front of Christ on the Cross and asking three simple questions:

- What have I done for Christ?
- What am I doing for Christ?
- What ought I to do for Christ?

He then says to pay attention to the answers that arise. He writes, "The Colloquy is made, properly speaking, as one friend speaks to another, or as a servant to his master; now asking some grace, now blaming oneself for some misdeed, now communicating one's affairs, and asking advice in them."[2]

Once I'm in that place with Christ, I continue to bring him my questions. He will sometimes gently take control over my imagination and reveal something to me through it. While these locutions are less spectacular than St. Paul getting knocked off his proverbial horse, my simple conversations with Christ transform my understanding of the dozens of little challenges I face each day. These "mini-visions" help me to see situations in a new way without any of the external factors changing. And they're the key to making God my hope, happiness, and fulfillment . . . no matter how long I wait for my next milestone.

ALLOWING GOD TO TAKE CONTROL OF MY IMAGINATION

Once, praying the prayer of surrender, I imagined putting my troubles into Jesus's hands. Jesus directed my attention to the nail holes in his palms. As I put each part of myself into his hands, all that he judged would be bad for me passed through the nail holes. They acted like a sieve. Everything that was good for me remained held in his hands. When I was finished with the prayer, he handed everything good back into my hands. It was so simple, but it changed my day. Shortly afterward the situation that needed resolution did resolve.

In another instance, I asked Jesus's help carrying my crosses for the day. I imagined my crosses on my shoulders, and they were crushing me. I cried out, "Jesus, why don't you take this away?" I instantly saw him directly in front of me, carrying his Cross too. I heard, "I am going before you in all things." There was peace accompanying those words. My cross wasn't going away, but I wasn't alone as I carried it. The way had been paved, and Jesus *understood* every aspect of my cross.

Another time, I struggled with anger over my lack of control of my life. I felt called to begin praying to Our Lady, Undoer of Knots. As I implored her to take care of my impossible situation, I could see my problem expressed as a tightly wound ball of string. There were so many loops, you couldn't see where they were all entering and exiting the knot. I identified how taut and tense I felt, like the string.

As I prayed, the string suddenly changed in its essence, becoming malleable and golden. The knot relaxed as if in relief, and the strings fell into a design. I was amazed at how beautiful the complex design was. It reminded me of intricate Celtic art-work, like those I had spied in the Book of Kells when I visited Ireland. The image communicated to me that not only could Our Lady take care of it, but by her intercession it would be transformed into something breathtakingly beautiful precisely *because* of how complex the problem had been.

In a recent instance, I was attempting to write a talk in a serious time crunch in the middle of a mini health crisis. I had trouble forming a sentence, let alone writing a forty-five-minute theological presentation! I struggled late one night to put any-thing worthy onto paper. Defeated, I just prayed and imagined myself in front of the crucifix. I imagined holding a box of all my jumbled thoughts. It was a poor offering, but I put it under Jesus's feet. The blood from his wounds dripped on the box, transforming everything inside. He said, "It's right where it needs to be. Now you can go to sleep." And as if by a small miracle, the talk got written and went superbly.

"GOD-INCIDENCES"

The "love notes" from God don't just happen in prayer. When I ask God for a sign of his love, he sometimes serves up cre-ative reminders in my day-to-day life. Once, walking through an empty hall in Grand Central Station on the way home after seeing friends, my familiar heartache started up. A man I hoped would be interested in me had been at the gathering earlier, and I clearly saw that he was interested in someone else. The disap-pointment was fresh in my heart, and I asked God to show me his love. Instantly, the sound of a mournful cello filled my ears.

I remembered how my choir director in college used to say the cello was the sound of a woman's heartstrings.

I ducked behind a phone booth where no one would see my tears, and I listened. The music understood me. Could it have been a coincidence that I heard the cello? Sure. But I wondered, *What kind of cellist plays to an empty hall?* I was the only person passing through, and the music had grabbed me as soon as I sent up my prayer. It felt like a private performance speaking directly to me.

Another time, I'd been mistreated by someone and had gotten into an argument with her. Neither of us had satisfaction, and I felt as if my heart had been rubbed on a cheese grater. I was trying to find peace and forgiveness in the swirling emotions, but it wasn't there. I asked God for a reminder of his love. Later that day a package arrived for me. A friend who makes jewelry sent me a necklace with the Sacred Heart of Jesus on it, totally unsolicited and out of the blue.

As I write this, I've been married for nearly eight years. The truth is, the ache of our hearts never goes away. No matter how saintly your spouse is (and mine is very saintly!), and no matter how deep your love is, married people still have many differences. No one can hold your heart perfectly except Jesus. My husband and I return daily to the Lord to ask for grace, understanding, and wisdom in our marriage. I haven't stopped needing reminders of the Lord's love and provision daily as I try to figure out how to navigate marriage and motherhood (states of life that don't exactly come with a manual!).

If God can orchestrate little reminders of his love, he can orchestrate the big events just as nimbly. Three hundred miles away, my husband was being prepared for me just as I was for him. Thank God every date and potential boyfriend didn't work out in those intervening months! My future husband was about to blow them all out of the water.

FORGETTING YOU'RE WAITING

Peace and trust in times of waiting become possible when we put real effort into seeking God's presence in our present circumstances. In times when he's doing background work we can't see, we need to remember that having him is the greatest reward. Not only will the waiting become bearable, but my hope is that you'll forget you're waiting at all!

St. Paul wrote, "I consider that the sufferings of this present time are as nothing compared with the glory to be revealed for us. . . . For I am convinced that neither death, nor life, nor angels, nor principalities, nor present things, nor future things, nor powers, nor height, nor depth, nor any other creature will be able to separate us from the love of God in Christ Jesus our Lord" (Romans 8:28, 38–39). We don't need to let the lack of the next milestone keep us from the love of the Lord.

YOUR ADVENTURE AWAITS: JOURNAL PROMPTS

Here are a few journal prompts for you to reflect on times of waiting in your own life.

⛰ Can you think of a time when you had to wait for something? In hindsight, can you think of any necessary benefits you acquired in that time of waiting—for example, certainty it was what you really wanted, maturity, or self-development to prepare you for having your prayer answered?

- Imagine God's perspective on your current time of waiting. What gifts is he trying to give you by making you wait? If you can't imagine any, bring that to him in prayer and ask him to show you—and to take care of your heart now.

- How is God sending you love notes in your current season—through people who speak his love to you, beauty in nature, opportunities for growth and challenge, "coincidences" that are really his creative gifts (for example, someone happening to bring you your favorite dessert on a tough day), his speaking to you in prayer, or in other ways?

- Have you fallen prey to believing that your happiness will come when you obtain a possession or achieve a milestone? What was the temptation—and what is the truth of the matter?

- Has God ever spoken to you by directing your imagination before? If not, I encourage you to try making a colloquy!

8

GOD, WILL YOU GIVE ME A SIGN?

HOW TO HEAR
GOD'S VOICE IN CONFUSION

Wait eagerly for the LORD, and keep his way;
He will raise you up to inherit the earth.
—Psalm 37:34

I was angry. Really angry. *Men!* I fumed. *Losers! No respect for my time or my heart, leaving me hanging!* This guy who was supposed to be coming to take me on a date was an hour and a half late. No call, no message, nothing. We had met on Catholic Match, and John was coming all the way from Pennsylvania to see me in New York, so I'd packed us a picnic lunch. We had planned to picnic in the rose garden and then go for a walk in my favorite park. If I liked him enough, I would invite him to Mass with my community members that evening, but if he was a no-go, then Mass would be my excuse to end the date. Clever, no?

Yet he didn't show up. I'd set aside my afternoon for nothing. There were no friends to ease the ache of loneliness. I ate my share of the picnic lunch and sat in self-pity. A few minutes later, I looked out my window and saw a car pull in. A slim figure jumped out, swung a backpack over his shoulder, and strode swiftly into the seminary. The receptionist called me: "There's a guy downstairs to meet you." I agreed to come down, but I took my sweet time doing so. This guy had already gotten off on the wrong footing with me . . . he could wait an extra few minutes after wasting ninety of mine.

I moseyed into the front office a bit later. The guy was standing, facing away from me. He turned around as I entered. The brow above his large brown eyes was furrowed in sincere sorrow. We made eye contact for a moment, and then he hung his head and whispered dejectedly, "I'm so sorry." I felt my stomach unexpectedly flip. *Oh my gosh, he's so cute.*

Reserving judgment and willing to hear him out, we strolled to the rose garden. It was easy to forgive in the halcyon April sunshine. It turned out John didn't own a cell phone, which explained why he hadn't called or texted that he was going to be late. He'd gotten terribly lost somewhere in the Bronx and, with no GPS to self-correct, had driven in circles for more than an hour before stumbling onto the Long Island Expressway. His handsome face and sincere apologies mollified my wounded pride.

John fascinated me. His ambition, if you can call it that, had been to enter religious life as a Carthusian, the most ascetic order in the world. John wanted to give his life to God in the most pure and total way possible. Ever seen or heard of the movie *Into Great Silence*? It's about the Carthusians who vow to talk socially only once a week, never leave their mountaintop cloister, abstain from meat their entire lives, and forego comforts such as HVAC in order to serve God in simplicity. That's the life John wanted . . . until he visited the Carthusians for two months. After he left, he never felt called back.

My fascination didn't end there. Not only did he not own a cell phone, but John also had no job and no car. Normally that would be an automatic no-go. However, his reasons piqued my interest even further. Shortly after leaving the Carthusians, John's grandfather passed away. His newly widowed grandmother experienced a health collapse and needed help. John went for what everyone thought would be a brief stay. A few weeks turned into a year and a half. John shopped, cooked, took care of the house, and ran errands for his grandma.

A year and a half! Although John humbly shrugged it off, saying he had no other plans for his life anyway, I knew he was extremely selfless. Would I have taken a year and a half off my own plans like that at age twenty-four? Probably not.

His grandma's health had recovered that spring, and he was getting ready to leave her house in Harrisburg, Pennsylvania, and head back to his hometown of State College. Here's the cool thing: I had set my maximum search radius on Catholic Match (CM) to three hundred miles from Long Island. If John had been home instead of serving his grandma, he would have been too far outside the search radius for us to find one another.

I'd been on CM for several months, and John's profile popped up for me the day he joined. I clicked on it and saw a few pictures as well as a self-portrait he'd painted of himself. He was really talented! I didn't know if CM would show my profile to John, so I decided to do a rare thing: I sent the first message. Just an emoji. Knowing that my energetic, type-A self could sometimes take the lead too much in a relationship, I resolved to allow him to lead and sent a mere emoji to let him know I existed. A modern-day "hanky drop," if you will.

Well, John responded very kindly and quickly with a desire to meet me. It turns out we are both unicyclists who love St. Thérèse of Lisieux. We both had a weird life . . . in oddly similar ways! Though not every woman would have appreciated such a bold approach of arranging to meet right away, I was tired of spending my evenings writing long messages to men I didn't know, so I happily accepted the invitation to meet in person.

The weather seemed to rejoice with us as we strolled through abundant meadows and along a beach bordering the Long Island Sound. John was unlike any man I'd ever met, but being with him felt natural. He wasn't desperately attaching to me and making me the measure of his self-worth. Nor was he holding me at a distance and examining me like a specimen under a microscope. He was pleasant, respectful, and an excellent listener. It turns out our date was the first one of his entire life.

As Mass drew near, I decided to invite him to accompany me—he made the cut!

At the end of the date, he gave me a hug and said that, if I was willing, he could borrow a car again to visit in a few weeks. He said he couldn't miss the opportunity to see me again. As I walked back inside to the seminary, I listened to the crickets chirping. I said aloud, "What a nice boy."

Later, I found out from John that he would have married me the day we met if he could have. Our courtship felt both natural and exciting. After many failed dates and ex-boyfriends, things just felt *right*. A mere six weeks after meeting, we began to date exclusively. Then, a month later—in July—a major milestone: John invited me to meet his extended family at their annual beach week on the Jersey Shore. I was ecstatic!

The day before departure I popped into one of the chapels in the seminary to offer thanksgiving. However, I experienced a vision that unnerved me: I saw myself as a nun in a habit. Fear seized me. *What if I haven't discerned my vocation correctly, and God has been calling me to religious life all along? Is this a sign I am on the wrong track?* Painful as it was, I knew I had to give God the first option in my life. I had to break the news of a potential breakup to John.

I drove to the beach with a heavy heart. The first opportunity that we had to be alone, I told him. He listened with peace in his eyes. I'm a great talker and he's a great listener, so I'm sure it took a long time! When I'd finally spilled everything, John took a deep breath. "Stacey," he said, "I love you, and I've never felt like I owned you. If God's calling you to be a nun, I'd be so happy to do whatever I can to help you get there."

That was it. No "But what about what I want?" No whining, clinging, or lashing out. His spiritual formation had taught him that he is a son of God. From that place of security, he could love sacrificially, even if it meant giving me up.

"Oh my gosh, you're so attractive." The words flew out of my mouth. I knew I really wanted to marry this guy. We went to Mass together the next morning and allowed ourselves to enjoy the time at the beach. John's peaceful reply had de-escalated my anxiety over the nagging question of my vocation. Was it a sign, or wasn't it?

GOD DOESN'T SEND US PUZZLES TO DECODE

I believe so-called signs from God are rarer in discernment than we'd like to believe. There are two reasons I believe this. The first is that often we don't even know what we're asking for, specifically. If God did send you a sign, how would you know what he was trying to communicate through it? It's too easy to begin looking for signs everywhere, and we can become obsessed with decoding potential signs.

I've seen a problematic trend in how some Catholics think about signs. I see people—good, earnest Catholics—who want a definitive direction about specific life choices, when very often God leaves the choosing up to us, as an expression of our free will. In such cases, asking for a sign can be a way of ducking responsibility for our lives.

There are times when we should ask for, and expect, answers! Especially when God has given us a specific task to do, and we are looking for open doors that will help us accomplish his will (as we find in the story of Gideon in Judges 6:36–40). But if we are looking for permission to do something contrary to scripture (such as dating an unbeliever—see 2 Corinthians 6:14), or we are simply afraid to step out in faith, we shouldn't wait for a sign!

As an example, let's imagine I ask God for a sign to show me whether I should marry John. Naturally I'm going to be on the lookout for signs everywhere. Perhaps I'm scrolling Facebook the next day and an ad comes up for a jeweler that sells wedding rings. Was that a sign from God or just targeted marketing? Or perhaps I'm reading the Bible the next day and I happen upon a story featuring John the Baptist. There's the name John! Was that my sign?

Do you see the problem? It's not that God can't or won't use signs. The problem is that, in asking him something nonspecific, I can automatically begin looking everywhere for confirmation of what I want to hear. Then God's answer becomes a matter of decoding a puzzle, which leads to distrust, rather than drawing closer to God and furthering my trust in him as I pray. By depending on arbitrary and often misleading signs, hearing God's voice becomes more like superstition than loving communication with our divine Father.

God is a good Father, so I can use my relationship with my earthly dad, who's also a good father, as a blueprint for communication with God. I asked my dad, "Do you think I should marry John?" My dad didn't say, "I'm going to send you a sign, but I won't tell you what the sign will be or when I'll send it. Just be on the lookout." He also didn't say, "You have to marry John or you're out of my will." Those answers would've been ridiculous! Instead, my dad wanted to aid me in making a wise decision. He said, "Tell me about different aspects of your relationship, and let's see if you and John are where you need to be to take the next step." When I had questions about how he and my mom knew they were called to marriage, he shared his stories and the wisdom he's learned over the years. He helped me sort through my motivations and questions. Ultimately, he left the decision up to me.

God treats us the way a good father treats his children. While I was upset at a lack of a definitive answer, God was parenting me the best way by letting me decide for myself.

READ THE WHOLE BOOK

One of the ways to discern a potential sign from God is to look at it in the context of your entire life. Using myself as an example, there are several reasons to believe that this momentary vision of myself in a nun's habit wasn't a direction from God. Looking at the context, I was living a sacramental life. I'd given God a year in discerning my vocation. I felt confirmed in prayer and by my spiritual director for months in my chosen path of marriage. My relationship with John was virtuous and inspired me toward greater virtue. Besides virtue, we shared a natural attraction for each other and my desires pointed solidly toward him. Therefore, seeing myself in a habit didn't make sense as a directive from God to enter the convent. It was a temptation to doubt and to disrupt my peace—a distraction.

Imagine picking up *The Lord of the Rings* trilogy and reading a single paragraph. Perhaps it's the paragraph where Faramir captures Frodo and Samwise on their way to Mordor. You read about their imprisonment and shut the book. Would it be accurate to tell people "I know *The Lord of the Rings* trilogy"? Absolutely not! You might draw the conclusion that Sam and Frodo never make it out of captivity, the Ring is never destroyed, and Middle-earth is doomed. You have to read the entire book to understand where that paragraph fits in the entire adventure. The same applies to our lives when we discern potential signs.

HOW WILL YOU KNOW?

Is it okay to ask God for a specific sign? I still wouldn't recommend discerning decisions that way. I once heard a story of a woman who was married but discerning divorcing her husband and marrying another man. She wasn't Catholic, so she didn't consider divorce and remarriage immoral. She went into a field of clover and prayed to God to let her find a four-leaf clover if she was called to marry someone else.

She looked down at her feet and found a five-leaf clover. Apparently, those are rarer than four-leaf clovers; your chance of finding one is one in one hundred thousand! As I was hearing the story I blurted out, "So she didn't marry the other guy, right? God didn't send her a four-leaf clover like she asked!" It turns out that the woman interpreted the five-leaf clover as double confirmation that she should marry the other guy, as if God were saying, "Don't *just* marry the other guy; marry him as soon as possible!" It made me sad to hear how she misinterpreted the "sign" to justify an unjustifiable choice.

Do you see the trap we set for ourselves by asking for signs, rather than listening for God's voice? If our ultimate vocation is heaven, and our highest aspiration is a relationship with the Lord, we must practice listening for God's voice to get the answers we need, waiting for the subtle whisper of the Holy Spirit or the peace accompanying daily mental prayer. We don't need to look outside ourselves for something dramatic that will foist the responsibility onto God to decide for us.

Sometimes the desire for a sign belies the wrong disposition of heart. While asking for a sign may feel like good discipleship, it can easily lead us to place the importance for an answer that

will satisfy our desire for safety above our relationship with God
himself.

God certainly can work through signs, and he has. Look
no further than the burning bush he sent to Moses! However,
I think a better path to hearing God speak is to invest regular,
daily time in study, scripture, and prayer. Always speak to your
spiritual director about any questions or doubts you have about
signs. He or she will help you see the threads of grace in your
life and where God is working.

If you're considering whether or not a potential sign came
from God, I've put together a list of questions to help you discern:

- Do I believe God's sign is telling me to do something that
  contradicts the teachings of the Church? (If so, disregard it.)
- Does the sign relate to my specific situation, or is it only tangentially relevant? (For example, receiving a wedding-dress
  boutique ad in the mail while discerning marriage would be
  tangentially relevant.)
- Where do I feel consolation and desolation? Does the sign
  fit into the context of those larger trends?
- If I had to make the choice entirely on my own, what does my
  gut instinct tell me? Does the sign align with that instinct?

As the days went on and I continued praying, I realized the
terrifying vision of myself in a habit hadn't come from God.
Within the context of my forward trajectory with John, it made
no sense for us to press pause on our relationship. Instead, we
joyfully continued discerning marriage together.

YOUR ADVENTURE AWAITS: JOURNAL PROMPTS

This chapter may have raised some underlying trust issues you have with the Lord. Use the following questions in your prayer time to discern if he's calling you to stop seeking a sign or an answer and instead lean into a relationship with him.

- The Bible says not to put God to the test (Luke 4:12). Do you feel anger at the Lord that you don't have a clear answer? If so, surrender that to the Lord and ask for his wisdom to help you see how loved you are.

- Does the Bible or *Catechism* have anything to say about the decision you are trying to make? As you talk about it with those whose counsel you trust, what is your gut telling you to do?

- Is this an opportunity to build up your relationship (or trust) in God? Do you feel as if God is playing tricks on you or setting traps to trip you up?

- Do you know how God's voice sounds when you're not discerning a decision, or do you only listen when you want something from him? If the latter, work on building a daily practice of spiritual reading (as outlined in chapter 1).

9

GOD NEVER TOLD ME WHAT TO DO

HEARING GOD'S VOICE IN PEACE

Peace I leave you; my peace I give to you.
—John 14:27

There was no question about it; my relationship with the once-wannabe monk was different than any I'd had before. Within a month of becoming exclusive, after knowing each other only three months, we were already deep in discussions of our vision for a future family. He was living in State College, Pennsylvania, and I was still in Huntington, Long Island, so we only saw each other on weekends. The weekdays positively dragged by, and our weekends seemed to fly.

I'd spent a few years living in England as a teenager because of my father's military career. I'd always wanted to return to Europe. Before I met John, I had a trip to England, Ireland, and Italy planned for late summer. When I planned it, I didn't know I'd be madly in love and spend my whole three-week vacation dreaming about returning to the States to see my man! I got to stay in a twelfth-century castle in Ireland, pray before the tomb of St. Francis of Assisi, and ascend the Scala Sancta in Rome, the stairs Jesus walked up to receive judgment from Pilate. Every place I went I thought, "I wish John were here with me."

One day, I took an unplanned diversion to a little town a half hour outside Rome named Calcata. It was a tiny medieval town built into a cliff. The houses hung precariously near and even over the steep drop, their balconies garnering spectacular mountain views. I wandered, amazed, through the main square and along the tiny streets, too narrow for cars to pass through. Eventually I sat down on a rocky crag and pulled out my journal. On this mountaintop I felt very close to God. This spot of wonder and joy felt like a great place to make big decisions. I whispered aloud to myself, "I'm going to marry John."

The freedom I felt that day was akin to what Adam and Eve must have felt in the garden before they chose sin. Indeed, it's the freedom God wants for his children when we make every one of our decisions. I'd explored religious life, loved and appreciated it, and wasn't running from it. I'd grappled with my past self-image issues and healed enough that I didn't need to latch on to John for security. I felt invited by John to be the best version of myself, and I was attracted to the beauty and purity I saw in his soul. After the messiness of my previous relationships, this one was a dream come true.

When I returned to the States, I headed straight for my family's house. I'd planned to leave New York and move back to Virginia to be closer to my family. John was going to meet them for the first time on my return. And I couldn't wait.

With my previous relationships, meeting my seven siblings and parents had been a kind of an initiation test. I would always watch the guy closely to see whether he could "handle" my noisy Italian people. With John, there was no initiation test. I felt such surety in the goodness of our relationship that I wasn't worried about whether he made a good first impression or not. I knew they'd come to know and love him in time.

My family saw the goodness in John right away. My littlest brother, Dan, who was only five at the time, immediately claimed him as an older brother. My sister Sue and I watched John walk across the backyard, patiently carrying a bucket of dirt for Dan to help build the end-of-the-world shelter he was casually constructing in a grove of trees. Sue observed, "John is making all of Dan's wildest dreams come true."

John arrived on a Friday to meet my family, and on Sunday he asked my dad if he could marry me. My dad was so surprised he said yes without thinking! Afterward, Dad asked me if I was okay with him giving his permission. As a girl who couldn't choose even items off a dinner menu without ruminating over it for twenty minutes, I was shocked at how quickly and definitively I responded yes!

The following weekend I visited John in State College. We attended evening Mass together, and I noticed something oddly shaped in his pocket. It was too thick to be a wallet or a phone. My heart nearly beat out of my chest, and I broke into a sweat. It had to be a ring box. After Mass, John asked me to take a walk with him. He took me to the newly unveiled Paterno chapel on campus at Penn State to show me a beautiful new crucifix. As we prayed, he went down on one knee and asked me to marry him. It was the easiest yes I've ever uttered.

After documenting my vocational discernment on world-wide television, my followers had the question: "How did God tell you his will for your vocation? How did you know?" My answer is that God never told me: he spoke through giving me peace.

I'd always thought decision-making had to be a long and laborious process. I'd been disappointed in my post-college years at how hard it was to discern religious life, heal from my self-image issues, and learn to surrender. Now I saw in hindsight that that background work had paved the way for an easy yes to marriage. John had the same experience in discerning religious life; although he wouldn't trade the experience of discernment, it was hard feeling lost, as if God was "breaking up" with him. The waiting and painful growth were completely worth it. Discerning religious life gave us spiritual maturity that would become a gift we'd give to each other.

God spoke in the peace in our relationship, and years later tears still well up in my eyes as I remember the incredible gift we have in each other. I always disliked when married people told me, "You'll know when you know." It felt as if they were in some elite club to which I'd never be admitted. But here I was now, admitting that my knowledge of my vocation was too deep to explain in words.

CHOOSING IN UNCERTAINTY

I count myself fortunate that marrying John was an easy decision, but I know it's not that quick or easy for many people. In my speaking ministry I've encountered countless young people searching for certainty of God's will in their choices. The desire to do God's will is a good one, and I commend them for it! However, I also caution them to be sure that they aren't subconsciously seeking *their own safety* under the guise of seeking God's will. Our anger when God doesn't reveal his will explicitly may well be the result of our not wanting to have to take responsibility for our choices.

Think of it this way: If God told you exactly what the plan was, you'd have perfect certainty it'd work out, right? And you could jump in with both feet, knowing success was certain. However, most of the time God doesn't intervene in our lives this way. As I've said many times in this book, he speaks almost exclusively to me about my *relationship* with him, not "the plan" for my life. It makes sense, since God isn't a to-do list. God is love.

I'm not saying your life choices aren't important. They are! It's just that often God wants us to do the work of discernment to gather data that will prove the right decision for ourselves. Giving us free will means he's not a helicopter parent.

In seeking God's will, I waited and waited for certainty. I thought there would be a sign or a vision. But it never came. Instead, I had to let the experience of true peace in my relationship with John be enough.

SWIM UPSTREAM: COMMIT!

In my opinion, American culture encourages irresponsibly extended adolescence. In Manhattan my church defined a "young adult" as someone age forty or younger. That's longer than the average lifespan (thirty-three) of the British population in Charles Dickens's day!

There are endless ways to distract ourselves and push off decisions because we're too busy filling up our calendar having fun. C. S. Lewis wrote:

> We are always falling in love or quarreling, looking for jobs or fearing to lose them, getting ill and recovering, following public affairs. If we let ourselves, we shall always be waiting for some distraction or other to end before we can really get down to our work. The only people who achieve much are those who want knowledge so badly that they seek it while the conditions are still unfavorable. Favorable conditions never come.[1]

This quote certainly doesn't apply to everyone, and I know there are many young adults encountering obstacles to their vocation over which they have no control. Still, I encountered a slew of unsolicited, bad advice over my choice to get married in my twenties. I was shocked when people on social media would authoritatively tell me I was too young to get married at age twenty-six because "I'm too young to know what I want." When in the world are we *supposed* to grow up, if not when we turn old enough to vote?

It's counterintuitive that narrowing your options by committing brings peace, but it does. In a world where the overwhelming advice is "Keep your options open," I can attest that letting go of lesser goods for a greater good leads to true peace. It gives you the opportunity to go deep, which is ultimately much more satisfying.

TRUE VERSUS FALSE PEACE

Recognizing true peace takes discernment. I remember a time when I hung up the phone on a family member in a moment of conflict instead of seeing the conversation through. I was scared to be vulnerable and reveal feelings that would have risked opening myself up to rejection. So, I made as fast an exit as possible, choosing to damage the relationship and cutting off the possibility of healing. The "peace" that resulted was really just relief that I got to stay safely high and dry out of conflict.

It didn't last, however. A nagging voice told me I hadn't done the right thing. You could call it—*Ding ding ding! That's right, ladies and gentlemen!*—the worm of discontent. My nobler, truer self knew that the less comfortable option of staying on the phone call and attempting to work through the conflict would have been the braver choice.

CONSOLATION VERSUS DESOLATION

Have you ever had a time when you wanted holy things? Prayer felt easy, you were motivated to pray, and you felt connected to God? That's called consolation. St. Ignatius writes about discerning the movements of your soul, and he writes that we have natural ups and downs in the spiritual life. Desolation is the opposite of consolation. I know those times too! Prayer is dry and feels difficult. Temptations keep knocking at the door seductively, begging to be indulged in for just a little while . . . and they're so hard to resist.

Sometimes God removes our consolation and replaces it with desolation for his own reasons. But sometimes neglecting prayer can be the cause of desolation. In either case, we should expect it and prepare for it. This life is a battle, no doubt, and respite we get along the way is a blessed break from the assaults of the enemy.

KNOW THE FRUITS

In Matthew 7:16–18 Jesus said, "By their fruits you will know them. Do people pick grapes from thornbushes, or figs from thistles? Just so, every good tree bears good fruit, and a rotten tree bears bad fruit. A good tree cannot bear bad fruit, nor can a rotten tree bear good fruit." A spiritual director or wise counselor—ideally, both—is invaluable to help you look at the fruits and determine whether your peace is true or false.

There is a kind of "false peace" we must guard against. If we are caught up in sensual delights of other forms of sin, we may experience a false peace because we are already under the devil's control. The devil never bothers the peace of someone already under his control. You must know the state of your soul. If you're going from mortal sin to mortal sin, it's easy for the devil to tempt you with a false sense of peace.

Ignatius tells us the good spirit will affect us by "pricking and biting" us with reason to try to shake us out of the false peace. Ignatius also points out that the converse can be true. When the soul experiences consolation from a good spirit, taking delight in the Lord, the devil may attempt to disrupt this peace with discouragement and obstacles. In attempting to take away the soul's peace, the evil spirit will actually spur us on "from good to better"!

The bottom line is simple: feelings, in and of themselves, are not as important as the fruit of that person's life, whether or not he or she is following wholeheartedly after God.

Looking at the fruits of my relationship with John gave me confirmation that the peace I felt about our relationship was real. First, we were each living a sacramental life in a state of grace, free from habitual mortal sin. Second, we felt mutually invited to be the most charitable, generous, and virtuous versions of ourselves. Unlike previous boyfriends who agreed to pursue chastity but slowly pushed the boundaries further and further, John took it upon himself to help me enforce the boundaries we'd agreed upon. That shared commitment showed me the strength of his character and built our mutual trust.

Our mutual love for consecrated life inspired us to write a charism for our future family, in order to live out our faith as intentionally as possible. A charism is what you might call a "plan of love." Religious orders have a charism that express-es their way of life and their particular values that help them uniquely live out their calls from God. We felt mutually inspired toward making a gift of ourselves.

This desire for self-gift is perhaps one of the best fruits you can have in a relationship. Pope Francis wrote beautifully in his exhortation *Christus Vivit*:

> These questions should be centered less on ourselves and our own inclinations, but on others, so that our discernment leads us to see our life in relation to their

lives. That is why I would remind you of the most important question of all. So often in life, we waste time asking ourselves: "Who am I?" You can keep asking, "Who am I?" for the rest of your lives. But the real question is: "For whom am I?" Of course, you are for God. But he has decided that you should also be for others, and he has given you many qualities, inclinations, gifts and charisms that are not for you, but to share with those around you. (no. 286)

DISCERN YOUR CHARISMS

John and I were inspired to write a family charism, thinking the only official expression of charisms was reserved for religious orders. However, years later we came to discover that the Church teaches that the Holy Spirit endows all baptized Christians with charisms and that an understanding of personal charisms goes all the way back to the early church. The *Catechism of the Catholic Church* states: "Whether extraordinary or simple or humble, charisms are graces of the Holy Spirit which directly benefit the Church, ordered as they are to her building up, to the good of men, and to the needs of the world" (799).

You may recall, if you've received the Sacrament of Confirmation, that the Holy Spirit gives seven gifts (wisdom, understanding, counsel, fortitude, knowledge, piety, and fear of the Lord) and that the result of those gifts are seven fruits (love, joy, peace, patience, kindness, goodness, and faithfulness). These gifts and fruits are distinct from charisms. One way to understand the difference is that the fruits and the gifts of the Spirit are given to you to keep (they become part of your character) while charisms are gifts given to you to give away (they are part of your mission). In other words, the gifts and fruits of the Holy Spirit are the "fuel" for carrying out your charisms.

So, what are the charisms? There are currently twenty-four charisms enumerated by St. Paul and St. Thomas Aquinas. I say currently because this list is not necessarily exhaustive. It's exciting for me to imagine how, as the world changes, the Holy Spirit could breathe new charisms into the work of baptized Christians for their mission. Here is a list of the charisms that have been defined so far:

- administration
- celibacy
- craftsmanship
- encouragement
- evangelism
- faith
- giving
- healing
- helping
- hospitality
- intercessory prayer
- knowledge
- leadership
- mercy
- missionary
- music
- pastoring
- prophecy
- service
- speaking in tongues
- teaching
- voluntary poverty
- wisdom
- writing

The Siena Institute has many helpful books and resources for those who wish discern their charisms in detail. For further scriptural reading, see St. Paul's writing in Romans chapter 12, 1 Corinthians chapter 13, and Ephesians chapter 4.

The Catechism states in paragraph 801 that discernment of charisms is necessary and always subject to the authority of the Church's shepherds. Your spiritual director or counselor should be able to help you understand your particular charisms. Your family and friends of faith can be a big help in an unofficial capacity, too. I recently hosted a gathering of Catholic women in my home and listed the charisms on a sheet with each lady's name at the top. We passed the sheets around and marked off the charisms we see manifested in each other. My friends loved it, and it challenged us to take the charisms others recognize more seriously as well as to look for new opportunities to express those gifts. It's by no means an exhaustive way to discern your charisms, but it could be a cost-free, fun exercise to begin your discernment. Often, others can see things about us that we can't, and their input can be invaluable.

Your charisms are gifts that should feel natural to you, that others can recognize as strong points, and that give you peace and joy to exercise. As I mentioned earlier, John and I wrote down our family charism when we were engaged (without knowledge of any formal discernment process or even the full list of charisms). Eight years into marriage, we've lived in three different states. In each place we've felt a calling and desire toward hospitality, even going so far as to invite forty people to a Christmas dinner party in our first tiny apartment of only six hundred square feet. These days in our bigger house, we truly enjoy inviting our entire friend group to just-because Sunday gatherings. We provide a simple main dish for everyone and ask families to bring a side dish or beverage to share. (To give you an idea of the usual size, I once told my kids that "only" eight families were able to make it. They slouched disappointedly, saying "that's nowhere near enough friends." I love that their version of normal is more like twelve to eighteen families!)

We feel joy cultivating our faith community here in the Shenandoah Valley, especially because we live in a hotspot for Catholics where new families appear in our parish every week.

As a former military brat who was always the new kid growing up, I feel a sense of peace and mission being radically hospitable to new families who are trying to get established. When I hosted my gathering for ladies, it didn't surprise me one bit that, according to them, hospitality was one of my most prominent charisms! Hopefully, my story will spark some ideas for you to identify yours.

YOUR ADVENTURE AWAITS: JOURNAL PROMPTS

With awareness of our natural positivity bias, we can use the following reflection questions to discern where God's peace is in our lives.

- When you imagine a potential path you may take, do you feel consolation? Consolation is a deep sense of challenge, invitation, growth, and expansion. (It may not make sense on the surface; for example, God may call you through consolation to make a shift to a lower-paying, but ultimately more rewarding, job.)

- Imagining a potential path, do you feel desolation? Desolation is a sense of disquiet, shrinking, shame, and a desire to hide.

- If you're discerning a relationship, take an honest look at the person you're becoming through that relationship. Are you inspired to become your "true self" as described in chapter 5? (The "true self" concept describes the noblest, most virtuous version of yourself.)

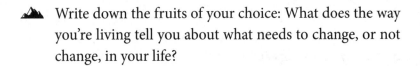 Write down the fruits of your choice: What does the way you're living tell you about what needs to change, or not change, in your life?

10

SEEING GOD IN YOUR STORY

THE 5-S'S OF A SURRENDERED HEART

> On my bed I remember you. On you I muse
> through the night for you have been my help.
> In the shadow of your wings I rejoice. My soul
> clings to you; your right hand holds me fast.
> —Psalm 63:6–8

Have you ever heard the saying "Be careful what you pray for; you might get what you want?" Well, God has a sense of humor, shattering all the timelines I thought I "had" to abide by. He brought me a spouse in record time—it took a mere five months between meeting my husband and sealing our engagement. And then, just three weeks after our wedding, even before we left on our honeymoon, we found out that our sweet son, a wedding night baby, was on the way!

We'd planned our honeymoon for two months after the wedding, so I spent our European trip eight weeks pregnant, nauseous and exhausted. Just three months after our first was born, we conceived another baby, a beautiful daughter. (I like to think we have a number of talents, but using Natural Family Planning apparently isn't one of them.)

By our second wedding anniversary John and I found ourselves somehow parenting boisterous "Irish twins," two children spaced less than a year apart. Caring for two tiny, energetic, beautiful humans was high adventure, indeed. My son took his first steps at just six months old, and he was climbing and running everywhere by seven months old. I found myself exhausted from chasing after him and wondered, *What have I gotten myself into?*

Any change, even good change, is perceived by the human brain as stress. And my life would be rife with change for several years! Being married to John was a joy, but motherhood was far more challenging than I'd anticipated. In a tough job market, John had to take a job in upstate New York. We didn't know a single person when we moved there. John worked three to eleven at night, which meant I, the former NYC socialite, was now confined to doing bedtime routine for the littles alone and then capping off my day in isolated silence.

I'd read somewhere that babies sleep eighteen hours a day. Not true. At five in the morning, they'd awake with screams in the pitch dark to begin our day. I'd always thought of myself as a really nice person. Now I discovered it was only because I'd enjoyed a full night's sleep most of my life. I was horrified at the resentful monster I'd become. Postpartum depression set in, and wallowing in self-pity became a habit. Long, harsh, dark upstate

New York winters didn't help. I was in shock at how I could love my children so fiercely and yet feel so angry.

Taking the babies to daily Mass was an absolute marathon. After a preparatory hour just to get out the door, I finally lugged my crew into church, laden with snacks and diaper bags and sweating profusely. They then proceeded to run laps around the church, whack their heads as they slipped on the marble floor, and screech. Forget ever hearing a homily again! Forget about feeling peace!

Starting with my engagement, big changes had been happening in my spiritual life. It was as if my "honeymoon phase" with the Lord came to an end just as my honeymoon with John was about to commence. I'd gotten used to visions in imaginative prayer almost daily, and they disappeared entirely. Prayer became dry and took effort. It felt as if God had suddenly fled and was ignoring me just when I most needed him in all the change.

I see now that God was inviting me to transition into a different, but no less valuable, phase of my spiritual life. The comparative silence lasted several years, through my engagement and into marriage. Can you blame me for wanting my visions to continue? If given the choice, wouldn't we all choose an easy, satisfying method of communicating with God? Yet I was being called out of comfort and into a season of self-gift. God loved me too much to allow me to become complacent in my spiritual life.

SILENCE ISN'T ABSENCE

Two years into marriage, I reached a breaking point. I wondered what I'd done to drive God's voice away and whether he'd ever speak to me again. I was angry with him for going silent just when I most needed his affirmation in the massive transitions to marriage and motherhood. I began speaking my sadness to a spiritual counselor. She helped me understand the larger landscape of what God was doing.

"Stacey," she said, "when God gave you all those consolations and visions, he was giving you the milk of comfort. Just like a baby needs milk that's easy to digest, he was making it easy for you to see his love. Nothing is wrong; you've now graduated to receiving the meat of a Christian life. It can be hard to chew and digest, but it's necessary in order for you to grow the way that God intends. Just as babies can't nurse forever, you also need to graduate to the next stage."

That conversation strengthened me. As I recalled the years since God's voice had vanished, the image of my engagement ring came to mind. Every day during my engagement I'd attend Mass. One day, I noticed my diamond caught the light in the church in a special way. It sparkled with a million scintillating facets, in a way it didn't sparkle anywhere else. From then on, I'd gaze at my ring in wonder every day in church.

Two years into marriage, I realized that God was like the light shining through my diamond. He was still just as involved in my life as he'd always been, whether I saw and heard him in church or not. As long as I stayed faithful to him and kept living a sacramental life, he could shine through me in a million ways. Now I had the opportunity to *be* holy through my service to my family rather than just *feeling* holy as I did in my single years.

St. Teresa of Avila writes that passing through the purgative way is necessary to enter the illuminative way. One of the components of the purgative way is aridity, a feeling of unfulfillment. Receiving no pleasure from good things we've previously enjoyed is one of the ways God reminds us that we're not meant to live here forever. It's a preparation for heaven. As St. Thérèse of Lisieux famously wrote, "The world is thy ship and not thy home."

Motherhood felt like a huge step backward spiritually, but it was actually a gigantic step forward. Gone were the days of a "perfect" prayer routine; now it was time to *be* Christ to my family and community. Instead of the validation of a cheering crowd after a show, I now had to learn to see the value in wiping little hands and bottoms and floors. The only gratitude I got some days was my tiny people's sweet hugs and kisses, after wiggling their way through diaper changes and turning their plates of food over onto the floor I'd just mopped! The opportunity to serve, not just from my abundance, but from my need—my exhaustion, my poverty of time and freedom—was an opportunity for greatness in the kingdom.

HEARING GOD SPEAK THROUGH OTHERS

In my years-long sadness at God for withdrawing his voice I missed a very important point: God had answered my prayers for a husband, and now I heard God's voice through him. One of the many things I love about John is his ability to give sincere, generous compliments. He praised my cooking, my sweetness to the children, my taking care of myself by working out, and my hard work to create a cozy and welcoming home.

He and I had spoken often in our engagement about wanting to become Christ to each other. Well, he was! I just didn't expect that John's affirmation would *replace* God's voice in my prayers. I wanted both. But when I stepped back and looked at how much love was coming to me, it was a beautiful sight. I was so validated and loved. God was loving me through John. It was really all about gaining an awareness, and then I could say, "Ah, okay, God, you didn't leave me—you just sent your messenger to tell me about your love."

MAKE ROOM FOR COEXISTING EMOTIONS

I felt like a jumbled mess. Didn't I have two beautiful children and a husband who loved me? Shouldn't I feel nothing but gratitude? It didn't help that so many people, even strangers at the grocery store, told me my young-motherhood years were "the best years" of my life.

I found I had new things to surrender as I prayed my trusty prayer of surrender. It became particularly difficult to surrender my expectations for the "perfect" prayer life I'd enjoyed as a single person. Once again, my trust in the Lord was being threatened as I struggled to get what I needed spiritually, socially, and physically. The solution that slowly emerged was learning the following basic principles:

1. God wants to be on my team.
2. God wants me to be on my own team too.

I was relearning, in a new way, the lessons I'd learned back in the days of my eating-disorder recovery. Guilt only worked against my well-being, and my family's too. I had to learn to understand what was *behind* the guilt, and then the emotions would become understandable. The spiritual counselor who told me about the milk of comfort also helped me learn to view myself with compassion. She advised me to name and write out the things I was grieving. I did, and I was amazed at how many things I felt I'd lost in all the change, even if only temporarily: My autonomy, my prayer time, my free time, my community, my ability to travel, my personal boundaries, my sleep, my dancing and singing . . . the list went on.

I began to be able to exercise compassion for myself and win the interior battle. Looking at the page of things that I felt I had lost, it became easy to sympathize with myself. Of course I was grieving! Well-meaning strangers were really commenting on *their own* lives, mirrored back to them by seeing my little ones. I slowly learned to just smile, thank them for their kind words, and move on with my day.

Over time, learning to hold grief and gratitude together allowed me to heal. As I moved through the grieving process of letting go of my former life, a new routine slowly emerged. I'd read scripture for just ten minutes at the beginning of my kids' nap time, and then talk to God informally for ten more min-utes. God knew I had lots to do, and he poured out the graces I needed when I disciplined myself to spend those first twenty precious minutes of my free time with him. Although I didn't hear his voice, I saw him working through the gift of his peace. My to-do list got done. I felt calmer. Usually, the babies napped long enough so I could get time to do something I enjoyed. I finally got to experience a new peace in the midst of surrender-ing my time and autonomy.

GOD'S ADVENTURE AWAITS

Time and time again, life will continue to change. I will always look heavenward in the rocking boat and cry out to God, "Are you still there? Will you still take care of me?" But it doesn't have to be a desperate plea. It can be a calm prayer, confident that God will come through.

I'm not the only person who's rocked by change. The ancient Israelite people were released from generations of slavery to the Egyptians. God ensured their freedom by sending plagues on the Egyptians, some of which were spectacularly gross, like the rivers turning to blood. He went before the Israelites in a pillar of fire, then parted the Red Sea so they could cross on dry land. It doesn't get more impressive than that!

And yet, after all of that, what did the Israelites do when the water ran short? They complained. They didn't trust, but instead wished to be back in Egypt. They actually mourned their slavery! Freedom was too big a change for them, and they wished for security, even if it meant giving up their freedom. The complaining and ingratitude dragged on time and again, even after God brought water from a rock and sent the perfect amount of manna to nourish them each day. They even fashioned themselves a golden calf to worship while Moses was away receiving the Ten Commandments.

Do these behaviors sound familiar to you? They sure do to me. When I'm in a tough season, how often am I tempted to complain, numb my emotions with online shopping or wine, or just ignore God and stop trying to pray? Haven't I seen enough evidence of his love to know he'll provide? Why do I keep demanding he reveal the plan to me in advance when scripture and experience show me that's not his way?

Unless you're given the rare gift of prophecy, you'll never, ever know the next step in your life ahead of time. In forty years of wanderings in the desert, the Israelites were never more than a week's journey from Canaan. It was their lack of faith in God that rendered them unable to step in and claim their promised land.

God doesn't want you to wander aimlessly in the desert for forty years. He wants you to trust him so you can make big leaps for his kingdom. If you're like me, you're probably more like a baby taking her first steps than a marathon runner. But, as my Irish twins have shown me, even a baby can get fast pretty quickly!

A PROACTIVE APPROACH TO OUR JOURNEY

When I teach voice students I tell them, "So much of good singing is thinking the right thoughts." My years of singing training have taught me a mental approach that helps me hit high notes on pitch. When the high note is a couple of bars away, I imagine myself on a cloud high in the sky. From there, I can "drop" down on the high note from above rather than trying to squeak my way up to it from below, which always results in coming in painfully under pitch. Approaching the challenging note from above mentally means that my body also follows suit in preparing: my lungs take a deeper breath, and my diaphragm supports with more power.

Besides thinking the right thoughts that lead to good technique, I have to discipline myself practically too. I practice breathing exercises to expand my lung capacity, learn the different resonating spaces in my body that produce a full sound, and challenge my range with vocal exercises.

We can approach our spiritual journey as a musician approaches singing. God is an adventurer and wants you to play a big game (aka hit the figurative high notes), so you'd better be ready for him to stretch you. This two-pronged approach, mental and practical, takes some explaining. I'll start with the practical side.

THE 5-S'S FORMULA—THE "SECRET SAUCE" FOR A SURRENDERED HEART

Decisions constantly need to be made, and they never end! The temptation to put my desire for the security of an answer will always be there, so I've come up with a little system to maximize my trust in God at every turn.

I've developed the 5-S's formula for spiritual health. Think of it as the "secret sauce" that will be your mainstay in all seasons of your spiritual journey:

- **Surrender:** In chapter 4 I enumerated the need for surrendering to God's will. Surrender requires trust and is the foremost prerequisite for a discerning heart and hearing God speak. Pray the prayer of surrender from chapter 4 daily (see page 47), identify which areas are a struggle for you that day, and intentionally surrender them (especially the difficult parts). The fruit you reap from this step will be immeasurable!

- **Study:** Become a lifelong student of your faith, using the method I detailed in chapter 1. Study and memorize scripture. Read the lives of the saints and the spiritual classics. Just fifteen minutes a day will keep you growing. Don't be afraid to silence all technology and give your spiritual reading full focus. The messages can wait fifteen minutes! Don't know where to start? In addition to my method for reading scripture detailed in chapter 1, I recommend *Divine Mercy in My Soul: The Diary of St. Faustina* as a jumping-off point.

- **Support:** You read in chapters 1, 2, and 5 how pivotal friends have been in my journey, both for better and for worse. Take an honest look at your friend group. Do they lift you up spiritually and encourage you in your journey? Or are you ashamed to mention your faith, or something in between those two extremes? I have found that even among groups who call themselves Christians there can be pervasive gossiping, exclusivity, and worldliness. If you need a friend upgrade, pray to the Holy Spirit for new friends or inspiration on how to be the light of change within your group. Also seek out and pray for mentors and a spiritual director, if you don't have one.

- **Silence:** In our distracted world, silence is the underrated key to wisdom. Times of silence allow the worm of discontent to speak and teach you about your heart's deepest desires. The best silence is with Jesus in the Blessed Sacrament. If you can, make a holy hour weekly or more often. One of my spiritual mentors used to tell me, "Just go and let Jesus love your heart." After an hour spent in his presence, I can attest that nothing compares to his peace.

- **Schedule:** In school my teacher always said, "Five minutes a day is better than an hour a week" for practicing math drills. In the same way, consistency is absolutely key in the spiritual life. As I shared in this chapter, it's important to welcome God into your day every day, not just relegating him to an hour for Mass on Sundays and a holy hour. I've also heard teachers say, "If you fail to plan, you plan to fail." While your current season may not allow you to make a holy hour every day, you should find time for at least fifteen minutes of daily quality time with the Lord. Remember that not all prayer is equal! I always prioritize scripture and silent time with God. Other wonderful devotions such as the Rosary, can be prayed as a family, while driving, or while I do housework; however, they don't check the box of my fifteen minutes of intimate prayer time with the Lord.

KNOW YOUR STORY

Let's turn now to the proactive mental approach I spoke of earlier, the spiritual parallel to approaching a high note from above in order to hit the note on pitch. My approach is more than an oversimplified "think positive!" mentality. To be honest, I cringe if someone dismissively tells me I can "think" my way out of a problem.

Instead, I present an evidence-based approach to anticipating challenges or fear over the next turn in the road. I call this approach knowing your story. It means noticing and calling to mind evidence of God's handprints in your past, in order to approach the future with trust in God. Knowing your story results from reflecting deeply on these questions:

- How has God spoken to me?
- Where has God come through for me?
- Where did God work something out for me in a way that I couldn't have done for myself?

You may not have dramatic examples of God in your life like those the Israelites received: the Red Sea parting to pave their path to freedom, or God appearing in a pillar of flame to guide them (see Exodus 13–14). However, as I've shared in previous chapters, God can speak in various ways. The same God who thought up sloths (which tells me he has creativity and a sense of humor) can for sure reach you in a way that's personal and distinct from anyone else. I invite you to look at your past through the spyglass of faith. Which of the following, if any, have you seen in your life?

- God answering prayers with results you've witnessed
- "God nods" of confirmation and affirmation
- God speaking through scripture
- God speaking in imaginative prayer
- God speaking to you through other people
- God giving you a voice or a vision
- God closing off an opportunity, which turned out to be for your greater good
- God speaking through true peace

As I write this book, looking back on my life so far solidifies in my mind the extraordinary love and faithfulness God has shown me. I'm willing to bet that, the longer and more deeply you shut off technology and look at your own story, seeking to see God in it, the more deeply you'll see his presence. Begin to think of your life as a masterpiece God is writing, and look for him in your story every day. Anxiety will subside and be replaced by gratitude. You'll act more proactively and wisely because you know it's not all up to you to make things happen. Surrendering to his will will become a part of the adventure.

There's something about this "storytelling" recollection of life that feels like watching one of my favorite movies, such as *The Lord of the Rings* trilogy. Frodo almost dies or is captured multiple times. He's doggedly determined, but circumstances make his mission seem impossible. But then, out of nowhere, deliverance comes! Gandalf resurrects from the dead and sends eagles to carry Frodo and Sam from the brink of death. The hidden effort and the struggle were all worth it to save Middle-earth.

You're the Frodo of your story. Although you and I may sometimes fall short of heroic or noble behavior, I still see a common theme in my story: like Gandalf, God loves to send his grace and save the day in a way I know I could never conjure up. That's how I know it's him. And recollecting his work gives me faith for my next steps.

In 1 Peter 3:15 we read, "Always be ready to give an explanation to anyone who asks you for a reason for your hope." Remembering and writing my story not only strengthens me, but it also becomes my testimony to give to the world. So, too, sharing your story will become the most effective tool for evangelization at your disposal!

WHAT IF I DON'T KNOW MY STORY?

I hope that reading my testimony in the previous chapters sparked memories of God's voice and provision in your life too. But maybe it didn't. Perhaps you don't know how to begin looking for his handprints, and you haven't heard his voice yet. Perhaps the memories of your past feel less like an adventure and more like a tragedy of shame or guilt.

A wide body of research shows that our brains hold on to past negative emotions out of self-protection.[1] Arising from basic instincts our ancestors needed to survive, this negativity bias keeps past criticism, trauma, and hurt at the forefront of our minds much more than past positive encouragement and meaningful connection. In modern days when we don't have the threat of being eaten or mauled by wild animals, we still have to fight against this survival tendency that filters out the good and remembers the bad.

With this in mind, seeing God in my story requires a long view and takes patience. Knowing that I'm more likely to think first of struggles and difficult moments, I give myself quiet and time to concentrate. I start with a particular season of my life and allow the memories to rise. I give them time to play out. When I think of my dad's cancer diagnosis, for example, the first thing that comes to mind is the fear I felt at possibly losing him. I remember the pit in my stomach as I saw him lose his hair and as my mom described his suffering during chemo. I cried a lot in that time, and nothing about the situation seemed divinely blessed.

Without dismissing the negative emotions, I give myself a little space to hold conflicting, true emotions as well. I intentionally ask myself, "Where did God show up here?" I remember the angels God sent: helpful moms who made meals for my family, became our prayer warriors, and dropped off presents at the door. I remember how petty fights with my siblings disappeared. The Thanksgiving dad was undergoing chemo, I felt closer to my family than ever before. In the end, God answered our prayers and healed my dad.

The more I see the fruits, the more I can see God in that chapter in my life. I saw Jesus in my dad, who suffered heroically without complaint. I don't take him or my other family members for granted the way I used to. God spoke through the love and concern of our community. I now find it easier to forgive faults I see in others. My family suffered, but we also experienced a little foretaste of heaven by loving one another more deeply and gaining a clearer focus on what's truly important. Last but not least, it's made me a more compassionate person because I know firsthand the complicated and difficult circumstances and emotions that medical diagnoses bring.

GETTING UNSTUCK

They say hindsight is twenty-twenty. I like to imagine God looking at the entire span of my life from above, as if from a hot air balloon, like the one pictured on the cover of this book. From that vantage point, I imagine him looking down at my life winding like a road through many twists and turns, peaks and valleys. He sees past, present, and future. Perhaps a valley that lasts a year feels like forever to me, but in his vision it looks short. Prayer is ascending with God to look down from his perspective. When I ask him, he sits with me and shows me the breathtaking beauty and grandeur I can't see when I'm stuck in a ditch below. It's freeing to recall that a different perspective, a more hopeful one, is possible and available to me when I pray. God doesn't dismiss the valleys and all the hurt that goes along with them. He instead raises us up to the beauty of the entire view.

You may have heard the sentence "God writes straight with crooked lines." Well, as you've read in the previous chapters, my life has felt like a series of hairpin turns. God's genius is the way he can use absolutely everything—even my sins—to lay a straight path. Reflecting deeply on my story, I see his deliverance through the hard moments, and it increases my trust in him to brave more hairpin turns.

Some of us have very deep valleys caused by trauma or abuse. In such cases it's always best, and often necessary, to process those parts of your story with a licensed therapist. In my experience a Catholic therapist is ideal, but any good therapist will still be of great help. If you have doubts about whether therapy is needed, I advise you to request an evaluation. God doesn't want you to feel as if your life is one never-ending valley.

YOUR ADVENTURE AWAITS: JOURNAL PROMPTS

Are you excited? I'm excited for you. Here is some trail mix for your journey in the form of journal prompts to get you started.

- List your spiritual and natural gifts. What are the ways you've been able to use them? What are you most proud of?

- What are you most grateful for? Imagine each thing as a gift from God, list it, and write "Thank you" next to it.

- Imagine a particular season of your life as if it were a chapter in a book. Write your story of that chapter, with you as the hero or heroine. Where did you struggle against temptation, and where did you triumph? What role did God play in that chapter?

- Where does God show up in your relationships? Does he act through receiving works of love from others, words of affirmation, or gifts, to name just a few?

- Have you ever seen God fulfill a promise he made through his words in scripture? If not, refer to the first chapter of this book and invest twenty minutes in reading scripture today. If he inspires any images or thoughts, write them down.

⛰ If you've been praying the prayer of surrender, what has been happening in your heart? Write it as though it's a chapter in a book. (I bet it's a cliffhanger!)

⛰ One storytelling pattern repeated over and over again in scripture is God showing up to save the day in an hour of desperation (think David defeating Goliath with a single rock). God loves to intervene in times that are beyond our control in order to show he's in control. Has he ever "saved the day" in your story? If so, how did it affect your faith? If not, be brave and invite him to do so.

⛰ What are your thoughts on the following verse: "We know that all things work for good for those who love God, who are called according to his purpose" (Romans 8:28). Do you believe that? If not, why not? Don't judge the belief you feel right now; it can be a helpful indicator of where you need to be delivered from a valley. Write out your thoughts in light of your story so far.

⛰ Have you ever received a God nod or felt the worm of discontent? How did it end up shaping that chapter of your story? Write it out as though you're the hero of the book.

⛰ What area(s) of the 5-S's formula do you need to work on? As a reminder, they are surrender, study, support, silence, and schedule.

God's adventure awaits, my friend!

NOTES

INTRODUCTION

1. "Resources," MR340.org, accessed December 2, 2024, https://mr340.org/resources/.

2. Pere Liagre, *A Retreat with Saint Thérèse* (Fitzwilliam, NH: Loreto Publications, 2014) 40.

2. ONIONS AND WORMS

1. C. S. Lewis, "The Weight of Glory," in *The Weight of Glory and Other Addresses* (New York: HarperCollins, 2001), 26.

2. Ignatius of Loyola, *The Spiritual Exercises of St. Ignatius of Loyola*, trans. Elder Mullan (New York: P.J. Kennedy and Sons, 1914), 14, https://ccel.org/ccel/ignatius/exercises.html.

3. Ignatius of Loyola, *The Spiritual Exercises*, 22.

4. VISIONS AND VOICES

1. Adapted from "Surrender Prayer," Prayers and Poems, St. Vincent's Catholic Church, accessed December 2, 2024, http://www.stvincentschurch.com/prayers-and-poems.html.

2. Teresa of Avila, *Interior Castle*, trans. John Dalton (London: T. Jones, Paternoster Row, 1852), https://www.carmelitemonks.org/vocation/StTeresa-TheInteriorCastle.pdf.

3. Jacques Philippe, *Searching for and Maintaining Peace* (Staten Island, NY: The Fathers and Brothers of the Society of St. Paul, 2002), 26–27.

4. Nina Strohminger, Joshua Knobe, and George Newman, "The True Self: A Psychological Concept Distinct From the Self," *Perspectives on Psychological Science* 12, no. 4 (2017): 551–560, https://doi.org/10.1177/1745691616689495. Examples of references to a "true self" in popular literature and movies abound, such as Shakespeare's entreaty, "To thine own self be true."

6. GOD WILL MEET YOU IN THE BIG DREAM

1. Marquette University, *Finding God in All Things: A Marquette Prayer Book* (Milwaukee, WI: Marquette University Press, 2005), 100. Used by permission of Marquette University Press.

7. LOVE NOTES IN THE WAITING

1. Pierre Teilhard de Chardin, *Hearts on Fire: Praying with Jesuits*, edited by Michael Harter (Chestnut Hill, MA: The Institute of Jesuit Sources, 1993, 2005).

2. Ignatius of Loyola, *The Spiritual Exercises*, 18.

9. GOD NEVER TOLD ME WHAT TO DO

1. C. S. Lewis, "Learning in War-Time," in *The Weight of Glory and Other Addresses* (New York, NY: Harper Collins, 2001), 60.

10. SEEING GOD IN YOUR STORY

1. Kendra Cherry, "What Is the Negativity Bias?" Verywell Mind, updated November 13, 2023, https://www.verywellmind.com/negative-bias-4589618.

STACEY SUMEREAU is a Catholic author and speaker, as well as the host of the *Called and Caffeinated* podcast and YouTube show. Previously, she performed in Broadway national tours of *The Wizard of Oz* and *Beauty and the Beast* and starred in the reality television show *The Sisterhood: Becoming Nuns.*

In 2020, Sumereau founded and hosted online conferences and courses—the Be Not Afraid conference, the God's Adventure Awaits summit, and the True North discernment course—to help people overcome anxiety, fear, and loneliness; develop decision-making skills; and discern their calling with clarity and peace.

Sumereau has contributed to the Ascension Presents YouTube channel and written for the *National Catholic Register*, *Vocations and Prayer* magazine, and LifeNews.com. She has presented at the National Catholic Youth Conference, the Los Angeles Religious Education Congress, and dioceses across the country.

She and her husband are raising their four children in the Washington, DC, area.

StaceySumereau.com
YouTube: @Seraphicallia
Facebook: @StaceySumereau
Instagram: @StaceySumereau

AVE
AVE MARIA PRESS

Founded in 1865, Ave Maria Press,
a ministry of the Congregation of
Holy Cross, is a Catholic publishing
company that serves the spiritual and
formative needs of the Church and its
schools, institutions, and ministers;
Christian individuals and families; and
others seeking spiritual nourishment.

———◆———

For a complete listing of titles from

Ave Maria Press

Sorin Books

Forest of Peace

Christian Classics

visit www.avemariapress.com

AVE MARIA PRESS
AVE Notre Dame, IN
A Ministry of the United States Province of Holy Cross